Lorilyn . Russell @ sas . com .

SAS® Programming Essentials for Educators

Course Notes

SAS® Programming Essentials for Educators Course Notes was developed by Kathy Kiraly, Lorilyn Russell, and Susan Walsh. Additional contributions were made by Elizabeth Ceranowski, Christopher Chan, Davetta Dunlap, Mike Kalt, Marissa Langford, Linda Mitterling, and Julie Petlick. Editing and production support was provided by the Curriculum Development and Support Department.

SAS and all other SAS Institute Inc. product or service names are registered trademarks or trademarks of SAS Institute Inc. in the USA and other countries. ® indicates USA registration. Other brand and product names are trademarks of their respective companies.

SAS® Programming Essentials for Educators Course Notes

Book code E70362, course code HECPES, prepared date 15Jun2007.   HECPES_001

Table of Contents

Course Description v

Prerequisites vi

Chapter 1   The DATA Step **1-1**

1.1   Structure of SAS Programs 1-3

1.2   SAS Data Sets 1-12

1.3   Creating a Permanent SAS Data Set 1-18

1.4   Writing a SAS DATA Step 1-24

1.5   Creating a DATA Step View 1-60

1.6   Solutions to Exercises 1-68

Chapter 2   Summarizing and Reporting Using SAS/GRAPH Software **2-1**

2.1   Writing SAS/GRAPH Code 2-3

2.2   Device Drivers (Self-Study) 2-34

2.3   Exercise Solutions 2-40

Chapter 3   Modifying SAS Data Sets **3-1**

3.1   Creating a SAS Data Set 3-3

3.2   Creating a New Variable 3-15

3.3   Using Conditional Logic to Create a New Variable 3-31

3.4   Using a Simple DO Loop to Process Data 3-47

3.5   SAS Array Processing 3-57

3.6   Subsetting Data Rows 3-70

3.7   Solutions to Exercises 3-82

Chapter 4   Working with Existing SAS Data Sets **4-1**

4.1   Concatenating and Interleaving SAS Data Sets 4-3

4.2   Match-Merging SAS Data Sets 4-15

4.3   Solutions to Exercises 4-26

Chapter 5   Accessing Data from Other Sources **5-1**

5.1   Accessing a Microsoft Excel Workbook 5-3

5.2   Creating a SAS Data Set Using the Import Wizard (Self-Study) 5-16

5.3   Solutions to Exercises 5-27

Chapter 6   Creating and Using Macro Variables **6-1**

6.1   Introduction to Macro Processing 6-3

6.2   Automatic Macro Variables 6-14

6.3   User-Defined Macro Variables 6-22

6.4   Solutions to Exercises 6-32

Chapter 7   Creating and Viewing SAS Data Sets with the SQL Procedure (Self-Study) 7-1

7.1   Creating a Report 7-3

7.2   Joining SAS Data Sets 7-7

7.3   Additional SQL Features 7-14

7.4   Solutions to Exercises 7-24

Appendix A   Index **A-1**

Course Description

This course provides students with the SAS knowledge and skills needed to more effectively use SAS software. Students create SAS data sets from raw data files, subset data, combine SAS data sets, create variables, use macro variables, and create simple graphs. This course is designed for professors who have no previous experience using SAS or who want to refresh their SAS programming skills.

To learn more...

A full curriculum of general and statistical instructor-based training is available at any of the Institute's training facilities. Institute instructors can also provide on-site training.

For information on other courses in the curriculum, contact the SAS Education Division at 1-800-333-7660, or send e-mail to training@sas.com. You can also find this information on the Web at support.sas.com/training/ as well as in the Training Course Catalog.

For a list of other SAS books that relate to the topics covered in this Course Notes, USA customers can contact our SAS Publishing Department at 1-800-727-3228 or send e-mail to sasbook@sas.com. Customers outside the USA, please contact your local SAS office.

Also, see the Publications Catalog on the Web at support.sas.com/pubs for a complete list of books and a convenient order form.

Prerequisites

Before attending this course, you should have at least six months of programming experience. Specifically, you should be able to

- understand file structures and system commands

- understand programming logic.

Chapter 1   The DATA Step

1.1   Structure of SAS Programs 1-3

1.2   SAS Data Sets 1-12

1.3   Creating a Permanent SAS Data Set...1-18

1.4   Writing a SAS DATA Step..1-24

1.5   Creating a DATA Step View 1-60

1.6   Solutions to Exercises 1-68

1.1 Structure of SAS Programs

Objectives

- Identify the components of a SAS program.
- Identify the components of a step.
- Review SAS program syntax rules.

3

Components of a SAS Program

A SAS program is a sequence of steps.

There are only two kinds of steps:

- DATA steps
- PROC steps

A SAS Program

DATA Step(s)   → Create SAS Data sets

PROC Step(s)

4

A SAS program can consist of the following:

- only DATA steps
- only PROC steps
- a combination of DATA steps and PROC steps in any order

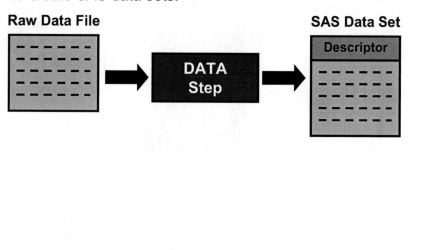

DATA steps can read the following:

- raw data files
- SAS data sets

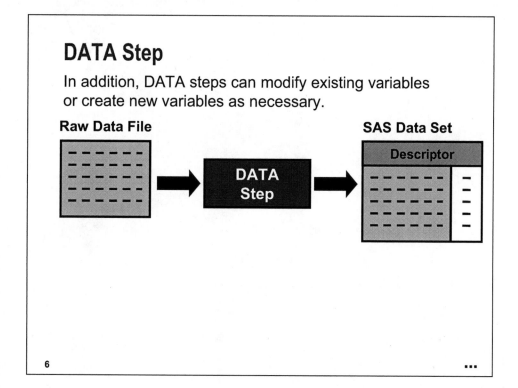

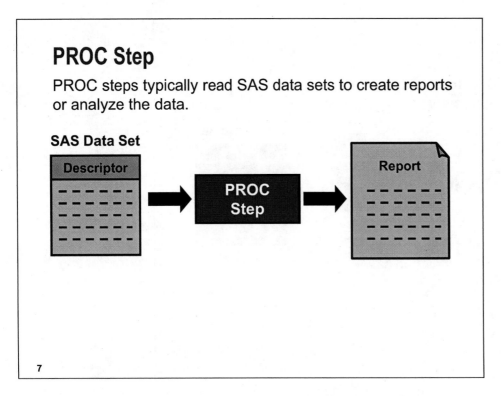

PROC Step

PROC steps typically read SAS data sets to create reports or analyze the data.

SAS Data Set

A PROC step invokes a prewritten program known as a *SAS procedure*.

The procedure automatically performs a processing function on the SAS data set.

Typically, PROC steps perform analyses and produce reports, although some procedures only create files.

Observations

PROC Step

There are many types of PROC steps.

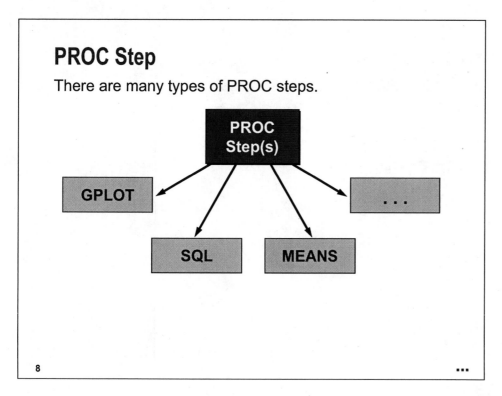

8

···

The output produced depends upon the procedure selected. The GPLOT procedure can generate plots of your data, while the SQL procedure can be used to create new tables, as well as reports. The MEANS procedure can generate descriptive statistics such as the mean, median, and standard deviation.

Components of a Step

A SAS program is a sequence of steps:

- DATA steps
- PROC steps

A *step* is a sequence of one or more statements.

9

Components of a Step

A *statement* usually starts with a keyword and always ends with a semicolon (;).

> **KEYWORD . . . ;**

10

Components of a DATA Step

A DATA step starts with a DATA statement and ends with a RUN statement.

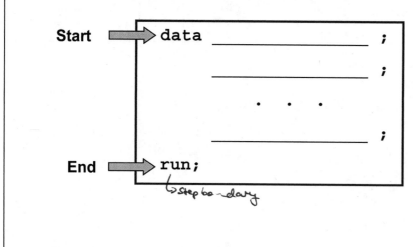

Start ⟹ data _____ ;

_____ ;

.   .   .

_____ ;

End ⟹ run;

↳ step boundary

11

The RUN statement is an explicit step boundary. It signals the end of the current step. A new DATA statement or a PROC statement can be used as an implied step boundary. Each step must have either an explicit or an implied step boundary in order for the program to process correctly.

Components of a PROC Step

A PROC step starts with a PROC statement and ends with a RUN statement.

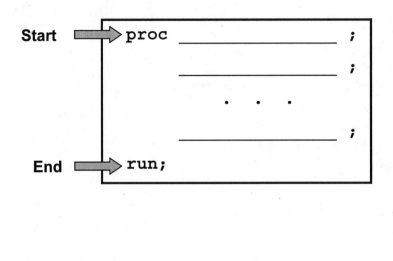

12

Some PROC steps that support run-group processing can end with a QUIT statement instead of a RUN statement.

SAS Syntax Rules

SAS statements are free format.

- They can begin and end in any column.
- One or more blanks or special characters can be used to separate words.
- A single statement can span multiple lines.
- Several statements can be on the same line.

```
data work.staff;
infile 'emplist.dat';    -> points to raw data file -> location
input EmpId $ 1-8 Name $ 10-37    -> setup structure of SAS dataset
JobTitle $ 41-62 Salary 82-88;
run;
    proc means data=work.staff mean max;
class JobTitle; var Salary; run;
```

13

SAS Syntax Rules

While not mandatory, simple spacing guidelines make
a SAS program easier to read.

```
data work.staff;
   infile 'emplist.dat';
   input EmpId $ 1 - 8 Name $ 10 - 37
         JobTitle $ 41 - 62 Salary 82 - 88;
run;

proc means data=work.staff mean max;
   class JobTitle;
   var Salary;
run;
```

14

SAS programming statements are easier to read if you

- begin DATA, PROC, and RUN statements in column one and indent the other statements
- put blank lines between programming steps.

SAS Syntax Rules

Adding comments to SAS programs helps others
understand what a program does and why.

```
   /* Create WORK.STAFF data set */
data work.staff;
   infile 'emplist.dat';
   input EmpId $ 1 - 8 Name $ 10 - 37
         JobTitle $ 41 - 62 Salary 82 - 88;
run;

  * Produce a listing report of WORK.STAFF;
proc print data=work.staff;
run;
```

15

Comments are typically used to document what a program does and why. Two methods are available in SAS for adding comments to a program. To use the first method, type

1. /*

2. *your comment*

3. */

To use the second method, type

1. *

2. *your comment*

3. ;

When you use the first method, avoid placing the /* comment symbols in columns 1 and 2. On some host systems, these symbols might be interpreted as a request to end the SAS job or session.

1.2   SAS Data Sets

Objectives

- Define a SAS data set and explain the descriptor portion and the data portion.
- Define a SAS variable.
- Identify a missing value and a SAS date value.
- State the naming conventions for SAS data sets and variables.

17

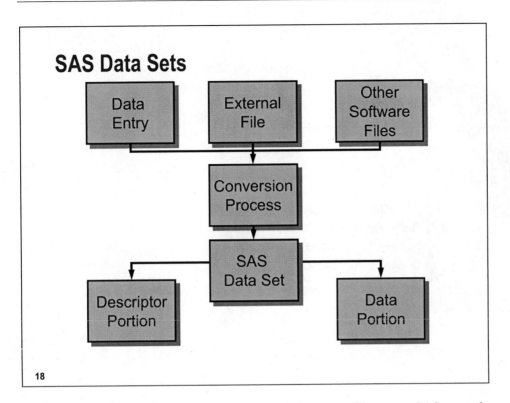

Data must be in the form of a SAS data set to be processed by many SAS procedures and some DATA step statements.

A *SAS data set* is a type of SAS file. A *SAS file* is a specially structured file that SAS software creates and organizes.

SAS Data Sets

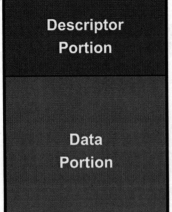

The **descriptor portion** contains attribute information about the data in a SAS data set.

The **data portion** contains the data values in the form of a rectangular table made up of observations and variables.

19

The descriptor portion of a SAS data set contains the following:

- general information about the SAS data set:
  - SAS data set name
  - date/time created
  - number of variables
  - number of observations
- attribute information for each variable in the SAS data set:
  - name
  - type
  - length
  - format
  - label

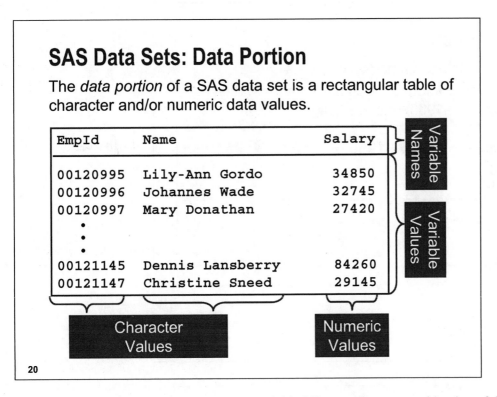

SAS Data Sets: Data Portion

The *data portion* of a SAS data set is a rectangular table of character and/or numeric data values.

EmpId	Name	Salary
00120995	Lily-Ann Gordo	34850
00120996	Johannes Wade	32745
00120997	Mary Donathan	27420
.		
.		
.		
00121145	Dennis Lansberry	84260
00121147	Christine Sneed	29145

Variable Names

Variable Values

Character Values

Numeric Values

20

A variable is considered to be a character variable if it contains any combination of the following:

- letters (A – Z, a – z)
- numbers (0 – 9)
- special characters (!, @, #, %, and so on)

Character variables can be 1 to 32,767 bytes long. Each character is stored as one byte. If the character value does not use the entire length of the variable, blanks are added to the end of the value.

Numeric variables can only contain numbers (0 – 9). They can also contain a

- decimal point (.)
- minus sign (-)
- letter E to indicate scientific notation.

A numeric variable is stored as a double-precision floating-point binary representation of the number. This storage method enables SAS to handle large and small numbers and provides precise mathematical manipulations.

SAS Date Values

SAS can store dates and times as numbers.

A *SAS date value* is interpreted as the number of days between January 1, 1960, and that date.

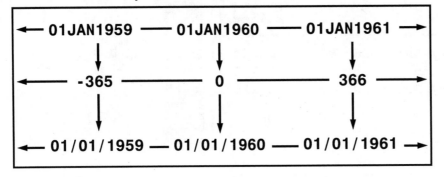

informat

Missing Data Values

A value must exist for every variable for each observation.
Missing values are valid values.

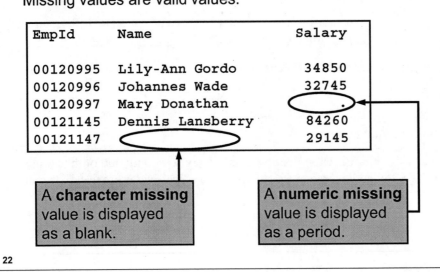

EmpId	Name	Salary
00120995	Lily-Ann Gordo	34850
00120996	Johannes Wade	32745
00120997	Mary Donathan	.
00121145	Dennis Lansberry	84260
00121147		29145

A **character missing** value is displayed as a blank.

A **numeric missing** value is displayed as a period.

Because of the tabular layout of the SAS data set, each observation must have a value for every variable.

Naming SAS Data Sets and Variables

SAS names

- can be 1 to 32 characters long.
- can be uppercase, lowercase, or mixed case.
- must start with a letter or underscore. Subsequent characters can be letters, underscores, or numeric digits.

23

Unix is case sensitive
SAS is not case sensitive

1.3   Creating a Permanent SAS Data Set

Objectives

- Explain the concept of a SAS data library.
- State the difference between a permanent library and a temporary library.
- Use the LIBNAME statement to create a permanent SAS library.

25

SAS Data Libraries

A **SAS data library** is a collection of SAS files that are recognized as a unit by SAS.

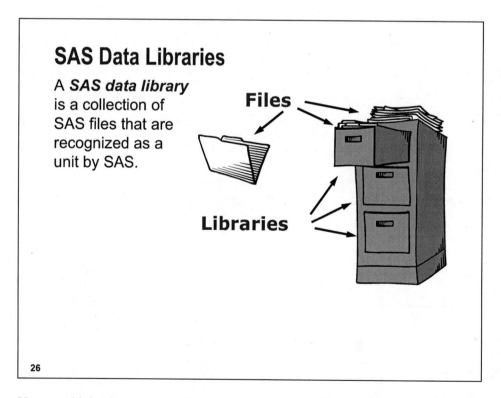

26

You can think of a SAS data library as a drawer in a filing cabinet and a SAS data set as one of the file folders in the drawer.

The library reference (*libref*) is a nickname for the physical location of the SAS data library.

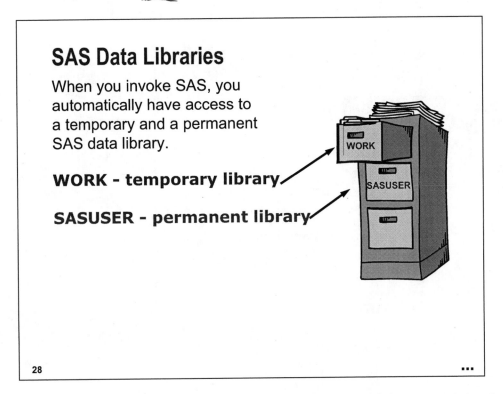

The SAS data sets stored in the temporary SAS data library WORK are deleted at the end of each SAS session.

SAS Data Libraries

Additional permanent libraries can also be accessed.

UNIV - permanent library

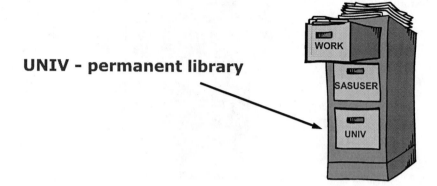

29   ...

SAS Data Libraries

A SAS data library is a collection of SAS files that are
recognized as a unit by SAS.

Operating Environment	SAS Data Library Organized As
Windows	directory
UNIX	directory
z/OS	specially formatted operating system file

30

The LIBNAME Statement

The LIBNAME statement can be used to access additional SAS data libraries.

General form of the LIBNAME statement:

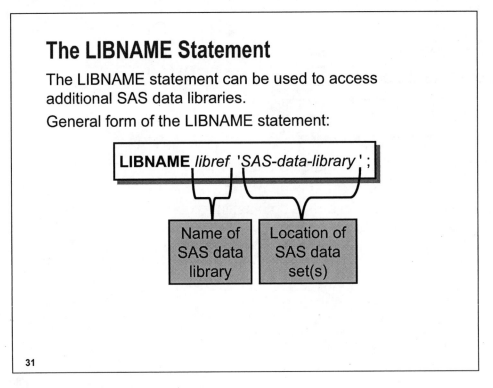

31

The LIBNAME statement is a global SAS statement. It is not part of a DATA step or a PROC step.

By default, the libref remains assigned until the end of the SAS session.

Each time that a SAS session is started, the libref must be reassigned for each SAS data library that is needed.

The LIBNAME Statement

Windows:
`libname univ 'c:\workshop\winsas\hecpes';`
UNIX:
`libname univ '/users/edu01/hecpes';`
z/OS:
`libname univ 'edu001.hecpes.sasdata';`

32

What Is a SAS Filename?

General form of a SAS filename:

> *libref.SAS-data-set-name*

libref   refers to the SAS data library
                               (library reference).

SAS-data-set-name   refers to a SAS data set in
                               the library.

33

What Is a SAS Filename?

The data set
customerorders
is a SAS file in the
univ data library.

The SAS filename is
univ.customerorders.

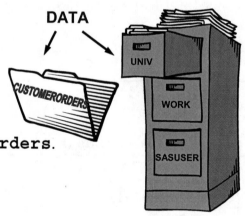

34

What Is a SAS Filename?

The libref work can be omitted when you refer to a file in the WORK library.

```
work.customerorders <-----> customerorders
```

35

1.4   Writing a SAS DATA Step

Objectives

- Understand the SAS DATA step.
- Write a DATA step to read nonstandard, fixed-column raw data.
- Explain the compilation and execution phases of the DATA step.
- Invoke SAS to enter and process a SAS program.
- View the descriptor and data portions of a SAS data set.

37

Purpose of the DATA Step

The DATA step
- names the SAS data set being created
- identifies the raw data file
- describes the fields in the raw data file
- reads a record from the raw data file
- processes the record
- writes the processed record to the SAS data set as a new observation.

38

The SAS DATA step converts a raw data file into a SAS data set. This conversion is necessary because SAS procedures require SAS data sets for analysis.

Business Need

Convert a raw data file into a SAS data set.

Partial Listing of Raw Data File:

```
029858  02JUN2001  1239347234  230100600005   4  130
029858  15JUL2001  1239686972  240800100020   1  122
029858  15JUL2001  1239686972  240800100036   1  468
029858  15JUL2001  1239686972  240800200009   1   87
029858  08SEP2001  1240124979  220200100116   1  181
```

39

The raw data file orders.dat must be converted into a SAS data set before it can be analyzed with SAS procedures.

The DATA Step

```
data _____ ;

    infile _____ ;

    input _____ ;

        .   .   .

run;
```

40

The DATA step begins with a DATA statement and ends with a RUN statement.

There are a number of additional statements that can be included as part of the DATA step. The DATA statement, the INFILE statement, the INPUT statement, and the RUN statement represent the minimum required to read a raw data file in order to create a SAS data set.

The statements must be specified in the order in which they appear above.

The DATA Statement

The DATA statement names the SAS data set being created and signals the beginning of the DATA step.

General form of the DATA statement:

DATA *SAS_data_set_name*;

Example:

```
data customerorders;
```

41

The keyword DATA begins the DATA statement. This is followed by at least one space and then the name of the SAS data set to be created, which is represented above by *SAS_data_set_name*.

The INFILE Statement

The INFILE statement names the raw data file to be read.

General form of the INFILE statement:

INFILE *'input-raw-data-file'*;

Example:

```
infile 'orders.dat';
```

42

A pathname might need to appear before the name of the raw data file.

The INPUT Statement

The INPUT statement describes the fields in the raw data file. General form of the INPUT statement with *formatted* input:

INPUT *pointer-control variable informat . . . ;*

Formatted input is used to read data values by

- moving the input pointer to the starting position of the field
- specifying a variable name
- specifying an informat.

43

Column input, named input, and list input can also be used to read raw data files. For a detailed discussion of the forms and uses of these alternative input styles, see *SAS®9 Language Reference: Concept*.

Reading Data Using Formatted Input

Formatted input is appropriate for reading

- data in fixed columns
- standard and nonstandard character and numeric data
- calendar values to be converted to SAS date values.

44

Reading Data Using Formatted Input

Pointer controls:

@*n*   moves the pointer to column *n*.

+*n*   moves the pointer *n* positions.

An *informat* specifies

- the width of the input field
- how to read the data values that are stored in the field.

45

What Is a SAS Informat?

An *informat* is an instruction that SAS uses to read data values.

SAS informats have the following form:

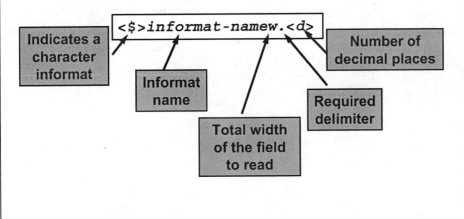

`<$>informat-namew.<d>`

Indicates a character informat

Informat name

Total width of the field to read

Required delimiter

Number of decimal places

46

Selected Informats

8. or 8.0   reads eight columns of numeric data.

Raw Data Value	Informat	SAS Data Value
1 2 3 4 5 6 7 →	8.0 →	1 2 3 4 5 6 7
1 2 3 4 . 5 6 7 →	8.0 →	1 2 3 4 . 5 6 7

8.2   reads eight columns of numeric data
and **may** insert a decimal point in the value.

Raw Data Value	Informat	SAS Data Value
1 2 3 4 5 6 7 →	8.2 →	1 2 3 4 5 . 6 7
1 2 3 4 . 5 6 7 →	8.2 →	1 2 3 4 . 5 6 7

47

Selected Informats

$8.   reads eight columns of character data and
removes leading blanks.

Raw Data Value	Informat	SAS Data Value
J A M E S →	$8. →	J A M E S

$CHAR8.   reads eight columns of character data and
preserves leading blanks.

Raw Data Value	Informat	SAS Data Value
J A M E S →	$CHAR8. →	J A M E S

48

Selected Informats

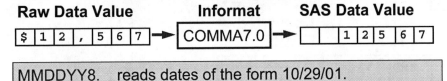

| COMMA7. | reads seven columns of numeric data and removes selected nonnumeric characters such as dollar signs and commas. |

Raw Data Value	Informat	SAS Data Value

| $ | 1 | 2 | , | 5 | 6 | 7 | → | COMMA7.0 | → | | | 1 | 2 | 5 | 6 | 7 |

| MMDDYY8. | reads dates of the form 10/29/01. |

Raw Data Value	Informat	SAS Data Value

| 1 | 0 | / | 2 | 9 | / | 0 | 1 | → | MMDDYY8. | → | | | 1 | 5 | 2 | 7 | 7 |

49

Working with Date Values

Date values that are stored as SAS dates are special numeric values.

A *SAS date value* is interpreted as the number of days between January 1, 1960, and a specific date.

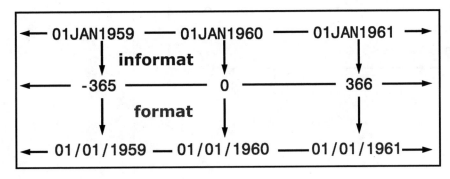

50

Convert Dates to SAS Date Values

SAS uses date **informats** to **read** and **convert** dates to SAS date values.

Examples:

Raw Data Value	Informat	Converted Value
10/29/2001	MMDDYY10.	15277
10/29/01	MMDDYY8.	15277
29OCT2001	DATE9.	15277
29/10/2001	DDMMYY10.	15277

Number of days between
01JAN1960 and 29OCT2001

51

The INPUT Statement

```
input @1 CustomerID $6.
      @8 OrderDate date9.
      @18 OrderID $10.
      @29 ProductID $12.
      @42 Quantity 3.
      @46 UnitPrice 3.;
```

58

The RUN Statement

The RUN statement signals the end of a step.

General form of the RUN statement:

```
RUN;
```

59

The DATA Step

General form of a complete DATA step with formatted input:

```
DATA SAS_data_set_name;
    INFILE 'input-raw-data-file';
    INPUT @n variable informat...;
RUN;
```

60

The DATA Step

Based on the business scenario, the syntax for the complete DATA step is as follows:

```
data customerorders;
   infile 'orders.dat';
   input @1 CustomerID $6.
         @8 OrderDate date9.
         @18 OrderID $10.
         @29 ProductID $12.
         @42 Quantity 3.
         @46 UnitPrice 3.;
run;
```

61

Compilation Phase

During the compilation phase of the DATA step,

1. code is checked for syntax errors

2. code is translated to machine code

3. an area of memory, called the *input buffer*, is established if SAS is reading raw data

4. an area of memory, known as the *Program Data Vector* (PDV), is established

5. required attributes are assigned to variables

6. the descriptor portion of the new data set is created.

62

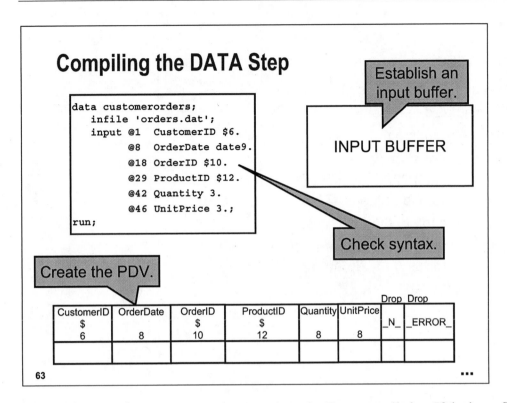

SAS determines whether or not to create an input buffer at compilation. If the input file is a raw data file, the input buffer is created. However, if the input file is a SAS data set, the input buffer is not created, and SAS writes the input data directly to the PDV.

The automatic variables _N_ and _ERROR_ are contained in the PDV, but are not written to the output SAS data set. The _N_ variable counts the number of times the DATA step begins to iterate. During each iteration, the _ERROR_ variable is set to 0 if no data error exists and is set to 1 if at least one data error occurs.

Execution Phase

During the execution phase of the DATA step,

1. the PDV is initialized to missing
2. data values are read into the PDV
3. other statements are executed
4. an observation in the PDV is written out to the output SAS data set at the end of the DATA step (by default)
5. SAS returns to the top of the DATA step
6. SAS initializes any variables that are not read from SAS data sets to missing (by default)
7. the process is repeated.

64

Executing the DATA Step

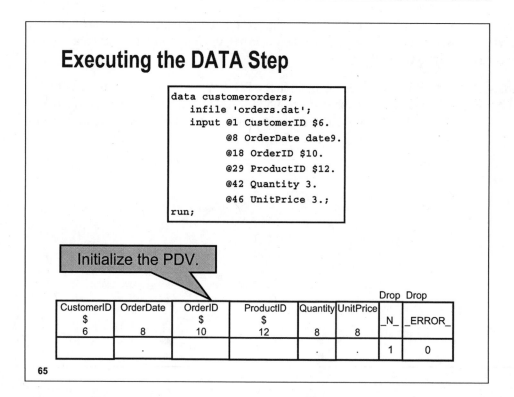

65

After compilation, variables in the PDV are initialized to missing except for _N_, which is set to 1, and _ERROR_, which is set to 0.

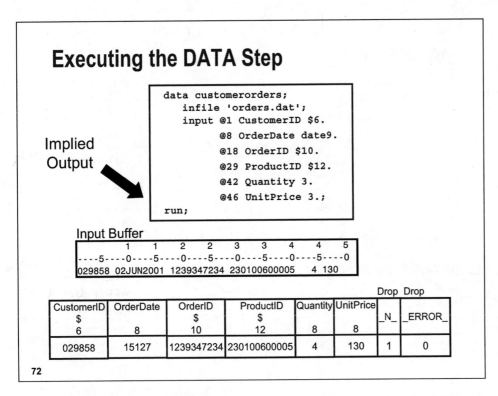

Executing the DATA Step

```
data customerorders;
   infile 'orders.dat';
   input @1 CustomerID $6.
         @8 OrderDate date9.
         @18 OrderID $10.
         @29 ProductID $12.
         @42 Quantity 3.
         @46 UnitPrice 3.;
run;
```

Implied
Output

Input Buffer

```
         1    1    2    2    3    3    4    4    5
----5----0----5----0----5----0----5----0----5----0
029858 02JUN2001 1239347234 230100600005    4 130
```

						Drop	Drop
CustomerID $ 6	OrderDate 8	OrderID $ 10	ProductID $ 12	Quantity 8	UnitPrice 8	_N_	_ERROR_
029858	15127	1239347234	230100600005	4	130	1	0

72

A record from the raw data file is read into the input buffer and the input pointer is positioned at the beginning of the data record. The INPUT statement reads data values from the record in the input buffer and writes them to the PDV. After the last executable statement in the DATA step, the values in the PDV, except those marked to be dropped, are written as one observation to the SAS data set.

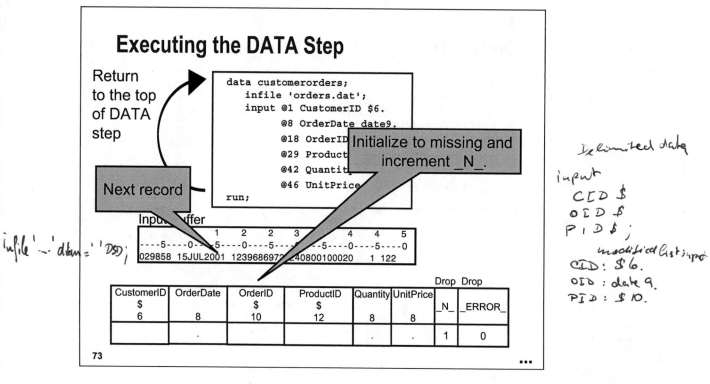

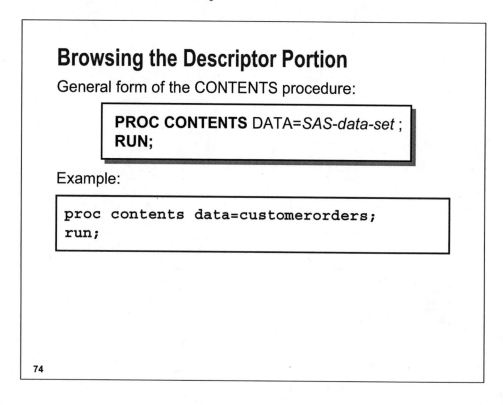

After the observation is written to the SAS data set, SAS returns to the DATA statement, the values in the PDV are initialized to missing, and _N_ is incremented by one. The next record is read from the raw data file into the input buffer. The second data record is written to the PDV, and at the bottom of the DATA step, the values in the PDV are written to the SAS data set. This process continues until SAS reaches the bottom of the input file.

Browsing the Descriptor Portion

General form of the CONTENTS procedure:

PROC CONTENTS DATA=*SAS-data-set* ;
RUN;

Example:

```
proc contents data=customerorders;
run;
```

74

Partial PROC CONTENTS Output

```
Data Set Name   WORK.CUSTOMERORDERS           Observations            201
Member Type     DATA                          Variables               6
Engine          V9                            Indexes                 0
Created         15:05 Friday, March 26, 2004  Observation Length      40
Last Modified   15:05 Friday, March 26, 2004  Deleted Observations    0
Protection                                    Compressed              NO
Data Set Type                                 Sorted                  NO
Label

        -----Alphabetic List of Variables and Attributes-----

            #     Variable      Type    Len

            1     CustomerID    Char      6
            2     OrderDate     Num       8
            3     OrderID       Char     10
            4     ProductID     Char     12
            5     Quantity      Num       8
            6     UnitPrice     Num       8
```

75

The descriptor portion of the SAS data set includes general information about the data set and attribute information about the variables in the SAS data set.

Browsing the Data Portion

General form of the PRINT procedure:

> **PROC PRINT** DATA=*SAS-data-set* ;
> **RUN**:

Example:

```
proc print data=customerorders;
run;
```

76

Several procedures can be used to generate a simple list report of the data in a SAS data set.
The PRINT procedure is one of the easiest and most often used procedures for this type of report.

PROC PRINT Output

Partial SAS Output

```
                                The SAS System

        Customer  Order                                           Unit
  Obs      ID     Date     OrderID       ProductID     Quantity   Price

    1     029858  15128   1239347234    230100600005      4        130
    2     029858  15171   1239686972    240800100020      1        122
    3     029858  15171   1239686972    240800100036      1        468
    4     029858  15171   1239686972    240800200009      1         87
    5     029858  15226   1240124979    220200100116      1        181
    6     029858  15265   1240437628    220200100179      1        135
    7     029858  15278   1240541766    240700100002      1         23
    8     030643  15129   1239353107    220101400204      2         19
    9     030643  15129   1239353107    220101400205      2         25
   10     031116  15333   1240981842    240100100550      2        132
```

77

✎   In the report above, the default date and page number have been suppressed with an OPTIONS statement.

General form of the OPTIONS statement:

OPTIONS option(s)…;

Selected SAS system options:

NODATE	specifies not to print the date and time the SAS session began. To turn the date back on, use the DATE option, which is the default.
NONUMBER	specifies that page numbers not be printed. To turn the page numbers back on, use the NUMBER option, which is the default.
PAGENO=n	specifies a beginning page number (n) for the next page of SAS output.
LINESIZE=width or LS=width PAGESIZE=n or PS=n	specifies the width (LS) and lines per page (PS) to use for the SAS log and SAS output.

Formatting Data Values

You can use SAS formats to change how data values are displayed.

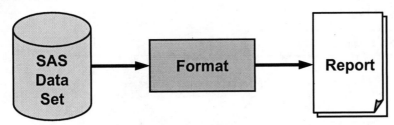

Values in the SAS data set are **not** changed.

78

Formatting Data Values

To apply a format to a specific SAS variable,
use the FORMAT statement.

General form of the FORMAT statement:

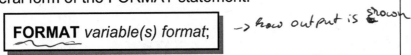

FORMAT *variable(s) format*;   → how output is shown

Example:

```
proc print data=customerorders;
   format OrderDate date9.;
run;
```

79

What Is a SAS Format?

A *format* is an instruction that SAS uses to write data values.

SAS formats have the following form:

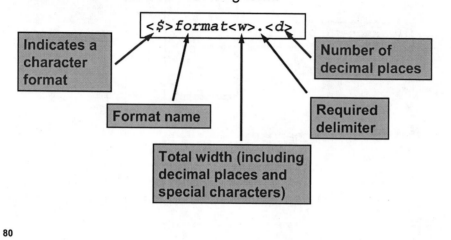

80

SAS Formats

Selected SAS formats:

w.d 8.2	standard numeric format Width=8, 2 decimal places: 12234.21
$*w.* $5.	standard character format Width=5: KATHY
COMMA*w.d* COMMA9.2	commas in a number Width=9, 2 decimal places: 12,234.21
DOLLAR*w.d* DOLLAR10.2	dollar signs and commas in a number Width=10, 2 decimal places: $12,234.21

81

SAS Formats

If you do not specify a format width large enough to accommodate a numeric value, the displayed value is automatically adjusted (rounded) to fit into the width.

Stored Value	Format	Displayed Value
27134.2864	COMMA12.2	27,134.29
27134.2864	12.2	27134.29
27134.2864	DOLLAR12.2	$27,134.29
27134.2864	DOLLAR9.2	$27134.29
27134.2864	DOLLAR8.2	27134.29
27134.2864	DOLLAR5.2	27134
27134.2864	DOLLAR4.2	27E3

82

SAS Formats

Recall that a SAS date is stored as the number of days between 01JAN1960 and the specified date.

SAS date formats display SAS date values in standard date forms.

Selected SAS date formats:

MMDDYY*w*.

Format	Displayed Value
MMDDYY6.	101601
MMDDYY8.	10/16/01
MMDDYY10.	10/16/2001

DATE*w*.

Format	Displayed Value
DATE7.	16OCT01
DATE9.	16OCT2001

83

SAS Formats

Examples:

Stored Value	Format	Displayed Value
0	MMDDYY8.	01/01/60
0	MMDDYY10.	01/01/1960
1	DATE9.	02JAN1960
-1	WORDDATE.	December 31, 1959
365	DDMMYY10.	31/12/1960
366	WEEKDATE.	Sunday, January 1, 1961

84

PROC PRINT Example Program

```
proc print data=customerorders;
    format OrderDate date9.;
run;
```

85

PROC PRINT Output

Partial SAS Output

			The SAS System			
Obs	Customer ID	OrderDate	OrderID	ProductID	Quantity	Unit Price
1	029858	02JUN2001	1239347234	230100600005	4	130
2	029858	15JUL2001	1239686972	240800100020	1	122
3	029858	15JUL2001	1239686972	240800100036	1	468
4	029858	15JUL2001	1239686972	240800200009	1	87
5	029858	08SEP2001	1240124979	220200100116	1	181
6	029858	17OCT2001	1240437628	220200100179	1	135
7	029858	30OCT2001	1240541766	240700100002	1	23
8	030643	03JUN2001	1239353107	220101400204	2	19
9	030643	03JUN2001	1239353107	220101400205	2	25
10	031116	24DEC2001	1240981842	240100100550	2	132

86

Assigning Column Labels

General form of the LABEL statement:

> **LABEL** *variable='label'*
> *variable='label'*;

'label' specifies a label of up to 256 characters.

Labels are used as follows:

- to replace variable names in SAS output
- automatically by many procedures
- by the PRINT procedure when the LABEL option is specified in the PROC PRINT statement

87

PROC PRINT Example Program

```
proc print data=customerorders label;
    format OrderDate date9.;
    label OrderDate = 'Date of Order'
          ProductID = 'Product ID';
run;
```

Needs to be on Proc statement

Split= ' ' → Date of Order

Split = '' → Date of Order*

88

PROC PRINT Output

Partial SAS Output

```
                           The SAS System

        Customer      Date of                                    Unit
Obs        ID          Order     OrderID      Product ID  Quantity Price

 1       029858      02JUN2001  1239347234  230100600005     4     130
 2       029858      15JUL2001  1239686972  240800100020     1     122
 3       029858      15JUL2001  1239686972  240800100036     1     468
 4       029858      15JUL2001  1239686972  240800200009     1      87
 5       029858      08SEP2001  1240124979  220200100116     1     181
 6       029858      17OCT2001  1240437628  220200100179     1     135
 7       029858      30OCT2001  1240541766  240700100002     1      23
 8       030643      03JUN2001  1239353107  220101400204     2      19
 9       030643      03JUN2001  1239353107  220101400205     2      25
10       031116      24DEC2001  1240981842  240100100550     2     132
11       031116      24DEC2001  1240981842  240100100618     2      84
12       032096      27JAN2001  1238338588  220100200011     1      63
13       032096      28MAR2001  1238815024  240500100017     1      54
```

89

Entering and Executing SAS Code

c01s4d1.sas

Enter a DATA step in the SAS windowing environment in order to create a SAS data set from the raw data file **orders.dat**.

1. Invoke SAS.

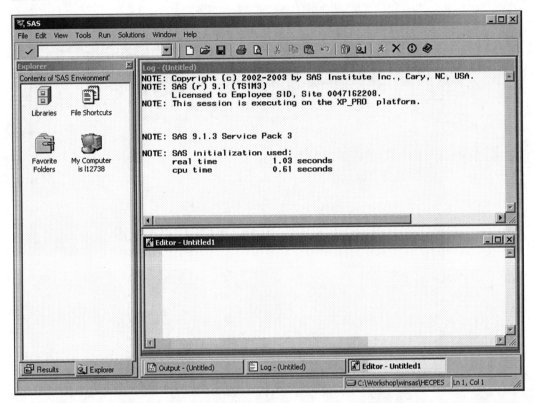

How you invoke SAS and the appearance of the SAS windowing environment varies by operating environment and by any customization in effect at a site.

By default in the Windows operating environment, the following windows are open:

- Results
- Explorer
- Output
- Log
- Enhanced Editor

The Enhanced Editor is only available in the Windows operating environment. The *Enhanced Editor* is an editor that uses visual aides to help you write and debug SAS programs. The Enhanced Editor includes many of the features from the Program Editor, plus additional features.

Details on the Results window, the Explorer window, and the Enhanced Editor window are discussed in a later section.

By default in the UNIX operating environment, the Program Editor window is open instead of the Enhanced Editor. All other windows that are open in Windows are also open in UNIX.

By default in the z/OS operating environment, only the following three windows are open:

- Output
- Log
- Program Editor

2. Close the Enhanced Editor window by selecting 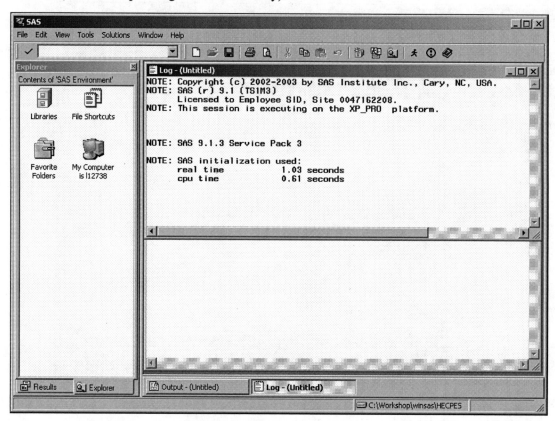 in the top-right corner of the Enhanced Editor window (Windows operating environment only).

3. Activate the Program Editor window by using one of the following methods:

   - Select **View** ➪ **Program Editor** from the pull-down menus.

   - Issue the PROGRAM command (can be abbreviated as PROG or PGM) on the command line or the command bar and press ENTER.

   - Select the appropriate function key.

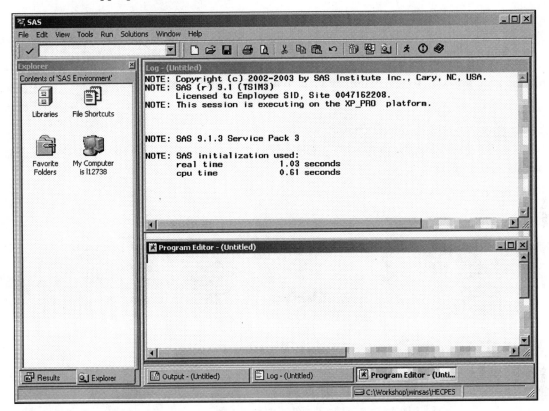

4. In the Program Editor window, type the following DATA step code that reads the raw data file orders.dat and creates the SAS data set **customerorders**.

```
data customerorders;
   infile 'orders.dat';
   input @1  CustomerID $6.
         @8  OrderDate date9.
         @18 OrderID $10.
         @29 ProductID $12.
         @42 Quantity 3.
         @46 UnitPrice 3.;
run;
```

SAS allows code to be entered in free format. SAS program statements can

   - begin and end in any column

   - be on the same line as other statements

   - extend over several physical lines

   - be in uppercase or lowercase.

While not mandatory, the SAS program code illustrated above represents a suggested standard. The suggested standard is as follows:

- Begin DATA, PROC, and RUN statements in column one.

- Indent all other statements by several columns for readability.

- Include only one statement per line.

Another suggested standard (illustrated above by the INPUT statement) is to define each SAS variable on a separate line and to align the beginning and ending position numbers. This can facilitate understanding and the modification of the INPUT statement.

5. Submit the program code for execution by using one of the following methods:

- Select the submit button 🏃.

- Select **Run** ⇨ **Submit** from the pull-down menus.

- Issue the SUBMIT command (can be abbreviated SUB) on the command line or the command bar and press ENTER.

- Press the appropriate function key.

All of these methods are not available in all operating environments.

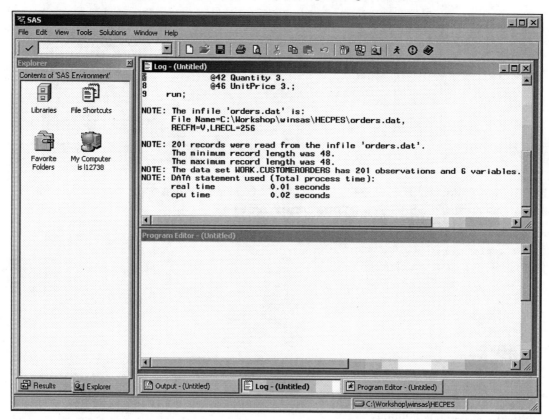

When program code is submitted in the Program Editor window, the window clears. However, SAS remembers the program code.

6. Activate the Log window and review the log by using one of the following methods:

- Click the mouse anywhere in the Log window if the Log window is open.
- Position the cursor anywhere within the Log window if the window is open and press ENTER.
- Select **View** ⇨ **Log** from the pull-down menus.
- Issue the LOG command on the command line or the command bar and press ENTER.
- Press the appropriate function key.

✐   All of these methods are not available in all operating environments.

The Log window

- is one of the primary windows and is open by default.
- acts as a record of your SAS session; messages are written to the log in the order in which they are generated by the program. You can issue the CLEAR command or select **Edit** ⇨ **Clear All** to clear the contents of the window.

The Log window contains the programming statements, as well as notes about

- any files that were read
- the records that were read
- the program execution and results.

In this example, the Log window contains no warning or error messages. If a program contains errors, relevant warning and error messages are also written to the SAS log.

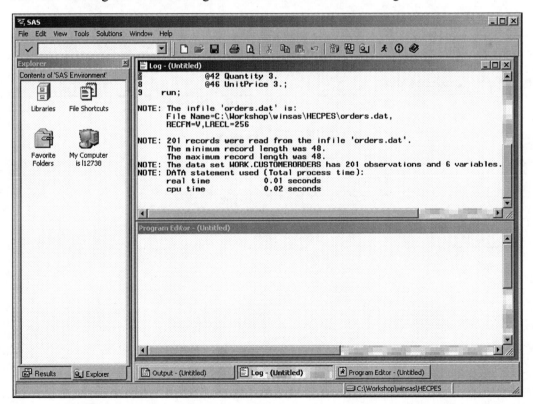

To review the log, use one of the following to view the entire contents of the Log window:

- scroll bars
- Page Up and Page Down keys
- appropriate function keys

✎ All of these are not available in all operating environments.

7. Add the PROC CONTENTS and PROC PRINT steps to the program to browse the SAS data set. Submit the code.

```
data customerorders;
   infile 'orders.dat';
   input @1  CustomerID $6.
         @8  OrderDate date9.
         @18 OrderID $10.
         @29 ProductID $12.
         @42 Quantity 3.
         @46 UnitPrice 3.;
run;

proc contents data=customerorders;
run;

proc print data=customerorders;
   format OrderDate date9.;
run;
```

8. Browse the output.

Partial CONTENTS Procedure Output

Alphabetic List of Variables and Attributes			
#	Variable	Type	Len
1	CustomerID	Char	6
2	OrderDate	Num	8
3	OrderID	Char	10
4	ProductID	Char	12
5	Quantity	Num	8
6	UnitPrice	Num	8

Partial PRINT Procedure Output

```
                                    The SAS System

              Customer                                                        Unit
     Obs         ID      OrderDate     OrderID        ProductID     Quantity  Price

       1       029858    02JUN2001    1239347234    230100600005        4       130
       2       029858    15JUL2001    1239686972    240800100020        1       122
       3       029858    15JUL2001    1239686972    240800100036        1       468
       4       029858    15JUL2001    1239686972    240800200009        1        87
       5       029858    08SEP2001    1240124979    220200100116        1       181
       6       029858    17OCT2001    1240437628    220200100179        1       135
       7       029858    30OCT2001    1240541766    240700100002        1        23
       8       030643    03JUN2001    1239353107    220101400204        2        19
       9       030643    03JUN2001    1239353107    220101400205        2        25
      10       031116    24DEC2001    1240981842    240100100550        2       132
      11       031116    24DEC2001    1240981842    240100100618        2        84
      12       032096    27JAN2001    1238338588    220100200011        1        63
      13       032096    28MAR2001    1238815024    240500100017        1        54
      14       032096    10APR2001    1238919361    210201000086        1        17
      15       032096    02MAY2001    1239097536    220200100046        1       116
      16       032096    08MAY2001    1239145649    220200300071        1       104
      17       032096    19JUL2001    1239719142    220100500026        2        63
      18       032096    19JUL2001    1239719142    220101400220        2        59
      19       032096    13AUG2001    1239914685    240500100061        3        78
```

9. Change the PROC PRINT step to use labels rather than variable names in the output. Submit the code.

```
proc print data=customerorders label;
   format OrderDate date9.;
   label OrderDate = 'Date of Order'
         ProductID = 'Product ID';
run;
```

10. Browse the output.

Partial SAS Output

```
                                    The SAS System

              Customer    Date of                                            Unit
     Obs         ID        Order       OrderID      Product ID    Quantity   Price

       1       029858    02JUN2001    1239347234    230100600005       4       130
       2       029858    15JUL2001    1239686972    240800100020       1       122
       3       029858    15JUL2001    1239686972    240800100036       1       468
       4       029858    15JUL2001    1239686972    240800200009       1        87
       5       029858    08SEP2001    1240124979    220200100116       1       181
       6       029858    17OCT2001    1240437628    220200100179       1       135
       7       029858    30OCT2001    1240541766    240700100002       1        23
       8       030643    03JUN2001    1239353107    220101400204       2        19
       9       030643    03JUN2001    1239353107    220101400205       2        25
      10       031116    24DEC2001    1240981842    240100100550       2       132
      11       031116    24DEC2001    1240981842    240100100618       2        84
      12       032096    27JAN2001    1238338588    220100200011       1        63
      13       032096    28MAR2001    1238815024    240500100017       1        54
```

11. Debug a SAS program with errors.

   a. In the Program Editor window, type the following SAS program. The program contains a syntax
       error: the word **data** is misspelled as **daat**.

```
daat customerorders;
   infile 'orders.dat';
   input @1 CustomerID $6.
         @8 OrderDate date9.
         @18 OrderID $10.
         @29 ProductID $12.
         @42 Quantity 3.
         @46 UnitPrice 3.;
run;
```

b. Submit the program. The SAS log contains the following message:

```
25    daat customerorders;
      ----
      14
WARNING 14-169: Assuming the symbol DATA was misspelled as daat.

26        infile 'orders.dat';
27        input @1 CustomerID $6.
28              @8 OrderDate date9.
29              @18 OrderID $10.
30              @29 ProductID $12.
31              @42 Quantity 3.
32              @46 UnitPrice 3.;
33    run;


NOTE: The infile 'orders.dat' is:
      File Name=C:\Workshop\winsas\HECPES\orders.dat,
      RECFM=V,LRECL=256


NOTE: 201 records were read from the infile 'orders.dat'.
      The minimum record length was 48.
      The maximum record length was 48.
NOTE: The data set WORK.CUSTOMERORDERS has 201 observations and 6
      variables.
NOTE: DATA statement used (Total process time):
      real time          0.00 seconds
      cpu time           0.01 seconds
```

The log indicates that SAS assumed that the keyword DATA was misspelled and executed the DATA step.

c. Use the RECALL command or select **Run** ⇨ **Recall Last Submit** to recall the program you submitted back to the Program Editor. The original program is copied into the Program Editor.

d. Edit the program.

1) Correct the spelling of data.

2) Remove the semicolon at the end of the DATA statement.

```
data customerorders
    infile 'orders.dat';
    input @1 CustomerID $6.
          @8 OrderDate date9.
          @18 OrderID $10.
          @29 ProductID $12.
          @42 Quantity 3.
          @46 UnitPrice 3.;
run;
```

e. Submit the program. Review the log and examine the error messages.

```
34    data customerorders
35        infile 'orders.dat';
36        input @1 CustomerID $6.
37              @8 OrderDate date9.
38              @18 OrderID $10.
39              @29 ProductID $12.
40              @42 Quantity 3.
41              @46 UnitPrice 3.;
42    run;


ERROR: No DATALINES or INFILE statement.
ERROR: Extension for physical file name "orders.dat" does not correspond
       to a valid member type.
NOTE: The SAS System stopped processing this step because of errors.
WARNING: The data set WORK.CUSTOMERORDERS may be incomplete.  When this
         step was stopped there were 0 observations and 6 variables.
WARNING: Data set WORK.CUSTOMERORDERS was not replaced because this step
         was stopped.
WARNING: The data set WORK.INFILE may be incomplete.  When this step was
         stopped there were 0 observations and 6 variables.
NOTE: DATA statement used (Total process time):
      real time           0.05 seconds
      cpu time            0.02 seconds
```

Notice the WARNING and ERROR messages.

SAS interpreted **infile** as the name of a SAS data set rather than as a keyword for the INFILE statement. The DATA step was not executed, so the existing version of **work.customerorders** was not replaced.

In other cases, the presence of syntax errors would lead SAS to underline and number the portion of the code that is in error and to print out numbered error messages (to facilitate the matching of error messages to errors).

12. Save your program.

a. Recall the program you submitted back to the Program Editor.

b. Edit the program by putting a semicolon at the end of the DATA statement.

c. You can use the FILE command to save your program to a file. The program must be in the Program Editor before you issue the FILE command.

Windows or UNIX: **file 'myprog.sas'**

You can also select **File** ⇨ **Save As**. A note appears that indicates the statements are saved to the file.

13. Submit a SAS program that contains unbalanced quotes.

    a.   Remove the closing quote from the INFILE statement.

    b.   Submit the program and browse the SAS log.

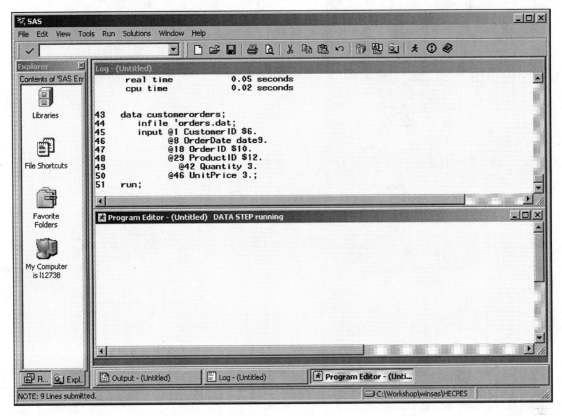

There are no notes in the SAS log because all of the SAS statements after the INFILE statement became part of the quoted string.

The banner on the window indicates the DATA step is still running because the RUN statement was not recognized.

There may be a WARNING message indicating that a closing quotation mark may be missing (for instance, you have an unbalanced quote).

14. To correct the problem in the Windows environment, press the Ctrl and Break keys.

15. Select **1. Cancel Submitted Statements** in the Tasking Manager window and select **OK**.

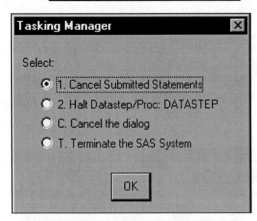

16. Select **Y to cancel submitted statements** in the BREAK -> Language Processor window and select **OK**.

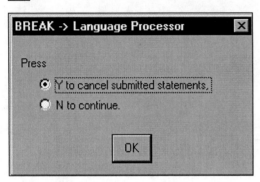

 **Exercises**

Write a DATA step that reads a raw data file containing information about the US employees at Orion Star Sports & Outdoors.

Fill in the blank with the location of the raw data file. Use an INFILE statement in a DATA step to read the raw data file named **employee.dat**.

```
data ...;
   infile '_____';
   .
   .
   .
```

The complete record layout for the raw data file is shown below.

Variable Name	Field Description	Columns	Data Type
EmployeeID	Employee Identification Number	1 - 8	Character
EmployeeName	Name of Employee	10 - 29	Character
JobTitle	Employee Job Title	32 - 53	Character
EmployeeDepartment	Employee Department	55 -70	Character
EmployeeGroup	Employee Group	72 - 96	Character
EmployeeManager	ID of Employee Manager	98 - 105	Character
Salary	Employee Annual Salary	107 - 113	Numeric
EmployeeHireDate	Date written in 12/31/2001 form	116 - 125	Numeric

1. **Reading Raw Data**

   a. Write a DATA step that creates a SAS data set named **empdata**. Use formatted input to create variables corresponding to each of the fields in the file layout above.

   b. After you run the program, read the log to answer the following questions:

      1) What is the name of the raw data file that was accessed? *employee.dat.*

      2) How many records were read from the raw data file? *73*

      3) How many observations does the resulting SAS data set contain? *73*

      4) How many variables does the resulting SAS data set contain? *8*

   c. Use PROC CONTENTS and PROC PRINT to display the descriptor and data portions of the data set. Print the dates in 31DEC2001 form.

   d. Recall your program and save it in a file named ch1ex1.sas.

1.5   Creating a DATA Step View

Objectives

- Investigate types of SAS data sets.
- Create and use DATA step views.
- Determine the advantages of DATA step views.
- Examine guidelines for using DATA step views.

93

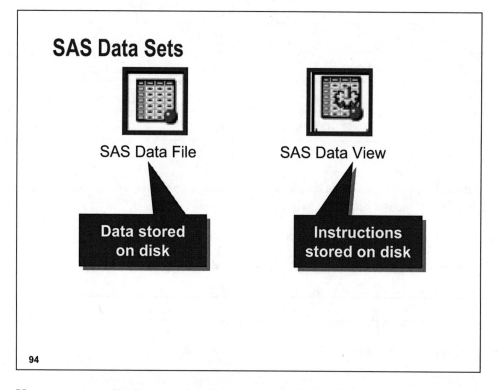

94

You can create a DATA step view instead of a SAS data file to read the raw data.

A DATA step file...	A DATA step view...
is a SAS file with a member type of DATA.	is a SAS file with a member type of VIEW.
enables read or write capabilities.	is read only.
contains data and a descriptor portion that are stored on disk.	contains no data.
	contains a partially compiled DATA step.

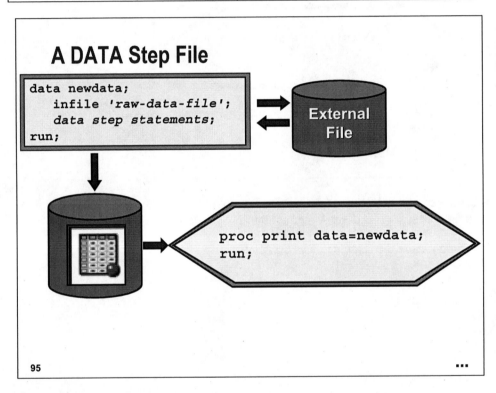

When a SAS data file is created, the DATA step is both compiled and executed.

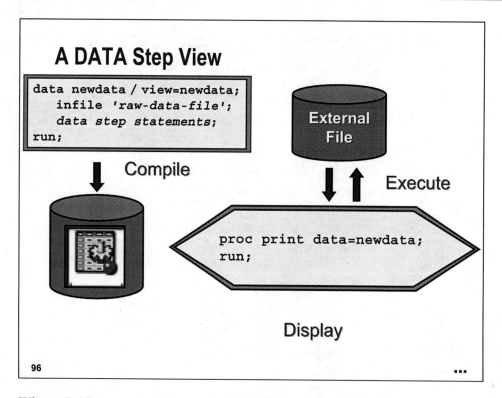

When a DATA step view is created, the DATA step is compiled but not executed. The DATA step is not executed until the data view is used in a procedure step or another DATA step.

A DATA step or SQL view cannot have the same name as a SAS data file.

DATA Statement with VIEW= Option Syntax

General form of the DATA statement with VIEW= option:

```
DATA data-set-name / VIEW=view-name;
     INFILE 'raw-data-file';
     INPUT variable specification...;
RUN;
```

view-name   specifies a view that the DATA step uses to store the input DATA step view. The *view-name* must match the *data-set-name*.

97

Use the DESCRIBE statement to display the source program that is stored in a SAS DATA step view. The results are listed in the SAS log.

General form of the DESCRIBE statement:

```
DATA VIEW=view-name;
     DESCRIBE;
RUN;
```

Creating a DATA Step View

c01s5d1.sas

The following code creates a DATA step view from the raw data file used in the previous demo:

```
data orders /view=orders;
   infile 'orders.dat';
   input @1  CustomerID $6.
         @8  OrderDate date9.
         @18 OrderID $10.
         @29 ProductID $12.
         @42 Quantity 3.
         @46 UnitPrice 3.;
run;
```

Partial SAS Log

```
43   data orders /view=orders;
44      infile 'orders.dat';
45      input @1  CustomerID $6.
46            @8  OrderDate date9.
47            @18 OrderID $10.
48            @29 ProductID $12.
49            @42 Quantity 3.
50            @46 UnitPrice 3.;
51   run;

NOTE: DATA STEP view saved on file WORK.ORDERS.
NOTE: A stored DATA STEP view cannot run under a different operating system.
NOTE: DATA statement used (Total process time):
      real time           0.13 seconds
      cpu time            0.02 seconds
```

Submit the following code to view the data, using the data view:

```
proc print data=orders;
   format OrderDate date9.;
run;
```

Partial SAS Log

```
52    proc print data=orders;
53       format OrderDate date9.;
54    run;

NOTE: The infile 'orders.dat' is:
      File Name=C:\workshop\winsas\hecpes\orders.dat,
      RECFM=V,LRECL=256

NOTE: 201 records were read from the infile 'orders.dat'.
      The minimum record length was 48.
      The maximum record length was 48.
NOTE: View WORK.ORDERS.VIEW used (Total process time):
      real time          0.12 seconds
      cpu time           0.00 seconds
NOTE: There were 201 observations read from the data set WORK.ORDERS.
NOTE: PROCEDURE PRINT used (Total process time):
      real time          0.25 seconds
      cpu time           0.03 seconds
```

Partial SAS Output

The SAS System

Obs	Customer ID	OrderDate	OrderID	ProductID	Quantity	Unit Price
1	029858	02JUN2001	1239347234	230100600005	4	130
2	029858	15JUL2001	1239686972	240800100020	1	122
3	029858	15JUL2001	1239686972	240800100036	1	468
4	029858	15JUL2001	1239686972	240800200009	1	87
5	029858	08SEP2001	1240124979	220200100116	1	181
6	029858	17OCT2001	1240437628	220200100179	1	135
7	029858	30OCT2001	1240541766	240700100002	1	23
8	030643	03JUN2001	1239353107	220101400204	2	19
9	030643	03JUN2001	1239353107	220101400205	2	25
10	031116	24DEC2001	1240981842	240100100550	2	132
11	031116	24DEC2001	1240981842	240100100618	2	84
12	032096	27JAN2001	1238338588	220100200011	1	63
13	032096	28MAR2001	1238815024	240500100017	1	54
14	032096	10APR2001	1238919361	210201000086	1	17
15	032096	02MAY2001	1239097536	220200100046	1	116
16	032096	08MAY2001	1239145649	220200300071	1	104
17	032096	19JUL2001	1239719142	220100500026	2	63
18	032096	19JUL2001	1239719142	220101400220	2	59
19	032096	13AUG2001	1239914685	240500100061	3	78
20	032096	13AUG2001	1239914685	240500200100	2	23

Advantages of DATA Step Views

You can use DATA step views to do the following:

- combine data from multiple sources
- hide complex code from users
- access the most current data in changing files
- avoid storing a copy of a large data file

99

Guidelines for Creating and Using Views

If data is used many times in one program, it is more efficient to create and reference a SAS data file than a view.

100

 **Exercises**

2. **Creating a Data View**

Open the program that you created in Exercise 1 (**ch1ex1.sas**) in the Editor window. You can also use the file named **bkup11.sas**.

a. Modify this program to create a DATA step view named **empdatview**.

b. Use the DATA step view that you created and PROC PRINT to produce a list report.

1.6   Solutions to Exercises

1. Reading Raw Data

a.   Write a DATA step to create a new data set named **empdata**.

```
data empdata;
   infile 'employee.dat';
   input @1   EmployeeID            $8.
         @10  EmployeeName          $20.
         @32  JobTitle              $22.
         @55  EmployeeDepartment    $16.
         @72  EmployeeGroup         $25.
         @98  EmployeeManager       $8.
         @107 Salary                7.
         @116 EmployeeHireDate      mmddyy10.;
 run;
```

b.   Read the log to answer the following questions:

   1) employee.dat

   2) 73 records read

   3) 73 observations

   4) 8 variables

c.   View the descriptor and data portions of the new data set.

```
proc contents data=empdata;
run;


proc print data=empdata;
   format EmployeeHireDate date9.;
run;
```

2. Creating a Data View

```
data empdatview /view=empdatview;
   infile 'employee.dat';
   input @1   EmployeeID           $8.
         @10  EmployeeName         $20.
         @32  JobTitle             $22.
         @55  EmployeeDepartment   $16.
         @72  EmployeeGroup        $25.
         @98  EmployeeManager      $8.
         @107 Salary               7.
         @116 EmployeeHireDate     mmddyy10.;
run;

proc print data=empdatview;
   format EmployeeHireDate date9.;
run;
```

Chapter 2   Summarizing and Reporting Using SAS/GRAPH Software

2.1   Writing SAS/GRAPH Code 2-3

2.2   Device Drivers (Self-Study) 2-34

2.3   Exercise Solutions 2-40

2.1 Writing SAS/GRAPH Code

Objectives

- Introduce SAS/GRAPH software.
- Introduce basic GCHART procedure and GPLOT procedure syntax.

3

Producing Graphical Reports

SAS/GRAPH software is the graphical presentation component of SAS. There are several ways to create graphical output with SAS/GRAPH. This course will introduce the use of SAS/GRAPH code using procedures such as GCHART and GPLOT.

4

The GCHART Procedure

General form of the PROC GCHART statement:

> **PROC GCHART** DATA=*SAS-data-set*;

Use one of these statements to specify the desired type of chart:

> **HBAR** *chart-variable* . . . *</options>*;
>
> **VBAR** *chart-variable* . . . *</options>*;
>
> **PIE** *chart-variable* . . . *</options>*;

5

When you use the GCHART procedure, perform the following tasks:

- Specify the physical form of the chart.
- Identify a chart variable that determines the number of bars or pie slices to create.
- Optionally identify an analysis variable to use for calculating statistics that determine the height (or length) of the bar or the size of the slice.

By default, the height, length, or size represents a frequency count (N).

✎   You can use HBAR3D, VBAR3D, and PIE3D statements to generate three-dimensional versions of these charts.

Chart Variable

The chart variable

- determines the number of bars or slices produced within a graph
- can be character or numeric.

6

Vertical Bar Chart

Produce a vertical bar chart that displays the number of employees in each department.

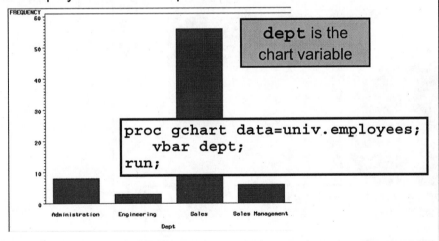

```
proc gchart data=univ.employees;
    vbar dept;
run;
```

dept is the chart variable

c02s1d1.sas

7

Horizontal Bar Chart

Produce a horizontal bar chart that displays the number
of employees in each department.

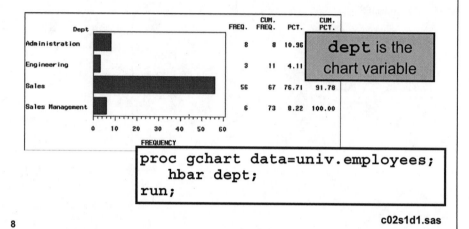

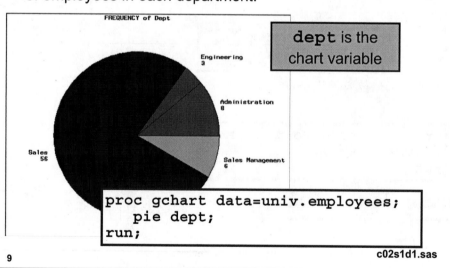

```
proc gchart data=univ.employees;
    hbar dept;
run;
```

8   c02s1d1.sas

Pie Chart

Produce a pie chart that displays the number
of employees in each department.

```
proc gchart data=univ.employees;
    pie dept;
run;
```

9   c02s1d1.sas

Creating Bar and Pie Charts

c02s1d1.sas

Assigning a Libref

1. Assign the **univ** libref to the permanent SAS library where the data sets for this course are stored.

```
libname univ '.';
```

2. Check the log to determine that the library has been successfully assigned.

SAS Log

```
1    libname univ '.';
NOTE: Libref UNIV was successfully assigned as follows:
     Engine:        V9
     Physical Name: C:\Workshop\winsas\HECPES
```

Creating Bar and Pie Charts

1. Use PROC GCHART to create a vertical bar chart of the number of employees in each department.

```
proc gchart data=univ.employees;
   vbar dept;
run;
```

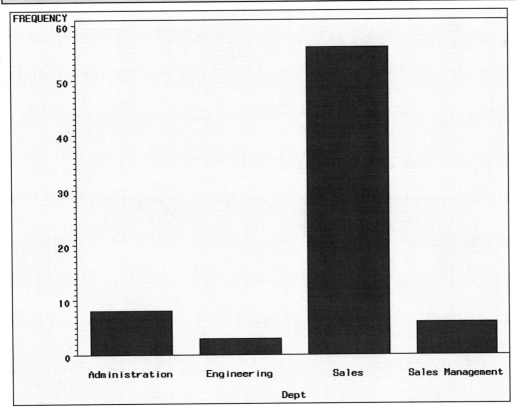

The chart shows that the Sales department has the most employees of any of the departments represented in the data set.

2.   Display the same information on a horizontal bar chart.

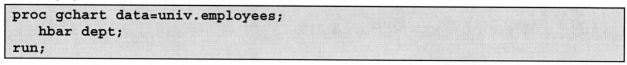

```
proc gchart data=univ.employees;
   hbar dept;
run;
```

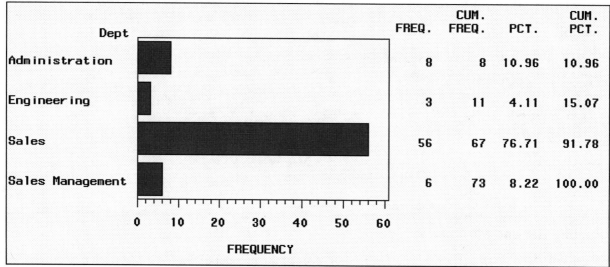

By default, a frequency table is displayed along with the horizontal bar chart.

3.   You can suppress the display of the frequency table by specifying the NOSTATS option in the HBAR
     statement.

```
proc gchart data=univ.employees;
   hbar dept / nostats;
run;
```

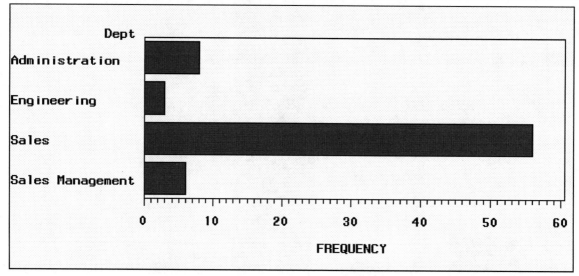

4. Generate a pie chart showing the same information (the number of employees in each department).

```
proc gchart data=univ.employees;
   pie dept;
run;
```

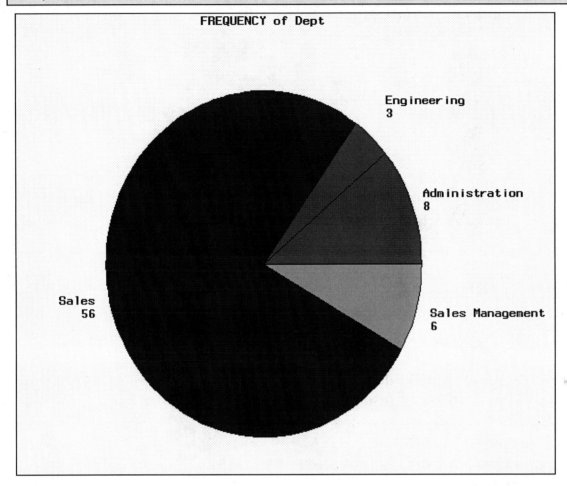

Character Chart Variable

If the chart variable is character, then a bar or slice is
created for each unique variable value.

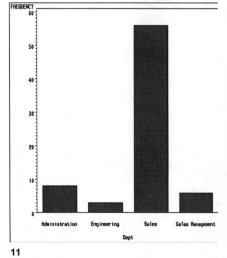

dept is the
chart variable

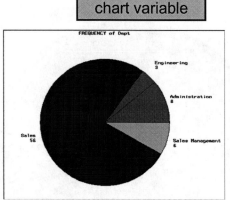

11

Numeric Chart Variable

For numeric chart variables, the variables are assumed
to be continuous unless otherwise specified.

The GCHART procedure creates the equivalent
of a histogram from the data.

- Intervals are automatically calculated and identified
  by midpoints.

- One bar or slice is constructed for each midpoint.

12

Numeric Chart Variable

Produce a vertical bar chart on the numeric variable
`YearsOnJob`.

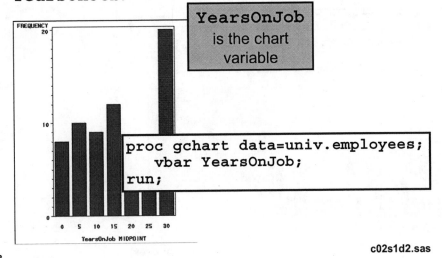

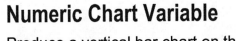
is the chart
variable

```
proc gchart data=univ.employees;
    vbar YearsOnJob;
run;
```

c02s1d2.sas

13

The DISCRETE Option

To override the default behavior for numeric chart
variables, use the DISCRETE option in the HBAR, VBAR,
or PIE statement.

The DISCRETE option produces a bar or slice for each
unique numeric variable value; the values are no longer
treated as intervals.

14

Numeric Chart Variable

Produce a vertical bar chart that displays a separate bar for each distinct value of the numeric variable `YearsonJob`.

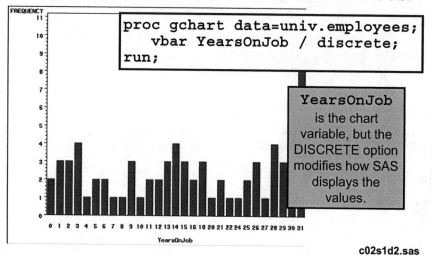

```
proc gchart data=univ.employees;
    vbar YearsOnJob / discrete;
run;
```

`YearsOnJob` is the chart variable, but the DISCRETE option modifies how SAS displays the values.

15   c02s1d2.sas

Summary Statistic

By default, the statistic that determines the length or height of each bar or size of pie slice is a frequency count (N).

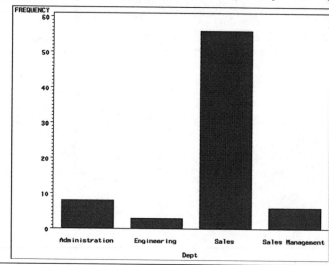

16

Analysis Variable

To override the default frequency count, you can use the following HBAR, VBAR, or PIE statement options:

SUMVAR=	identifies the analysis variable to use for the sum or mean calculation.
TYPE=	specifies that the height or length of the bar or size of the slice represents a mean or sum of the *analysis-variable* values.

If an analysis variable is

- specified, the default value of TYPE is SUM=
- not specified, the default value of TYPE is FREQ=.

17

Analysis Variable

Produce a vertical bar chart that displays the average salary of employees in each department.

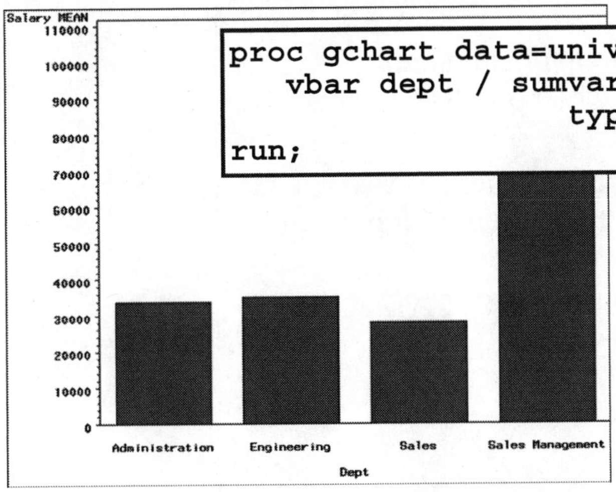


```
proc gchart data=univ.employees;
   vbar dept / sumvar=salary
                     type=mean;
run;
```

c02s1d2.sas

18

Bar Chart Using Formats

Produce a bar chart that displays the average salary
of employees in each department.

```
proc gchart data=univ.employees;
   vbar dept / sumvar=Salary type=mean;
   format Salary dollar8.;
run;
```

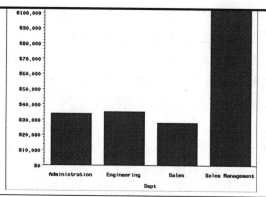

19   c02s1d2.sas

Run-Group Processing

PROC GCHART and many other SAS/GRAPH
procedures support run-group processing, which indicates
the following:

- The procedure executes the group of statements
  following the PROC statement when a RUN statement
  is encountered.

- Additional statements followed by another RUN
  statement can be submitted without resubmitting
  the PROC statement.

- The procedure stays active until a PROC, DATA,
  or QUIT statement is encountered.

20

Titles and Footnotes

You can use TITLE and FOOTNOTE statement options to modify the characteristics of text strings.

Selected options:

COLOR = *color* | C=*color*
FONT = *type-font* | F=*type-font*
HEIGHT = *n* | H=*n*

21

 **Using Bar Chart Options**

c02s1d2.sas

1. Create a vertical bar chart on the numeric variable **YearsOnJob**. Include a green title in the output.

```
proc gchart data=univ.employees;
   vbar yearsonjob;
   title color=green 'Number of Years on the Job for Employees';
run;
```

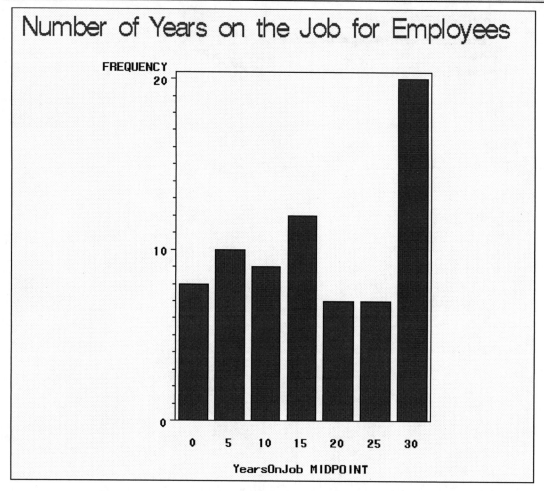

SAS automatically divided the data into seven intervals and shows the midpoint of each of the intervals. The information displayed is the number of employees who have years on the job falling within each interval. For example, each interval in this case represents 5 years. The second bar in the chart is the interval with a midpoint of 5, and therefore has a minimum value of 2.5 and a maximum value of 7.5. Therefore, there were 10 employees who have between 2.5 and 7.5 years on the job.

2. Modify the bar chart to have one bar for each unique value of **YearsOnJob** and to include a subtitle.

```
    vbar yearsonjob / discrete;
    title2 'as of December 2002';
run;
```

✎ It is not necessary to include another PROC GCHART statement in this program before the
VBAR statement because of RUN-group processing.

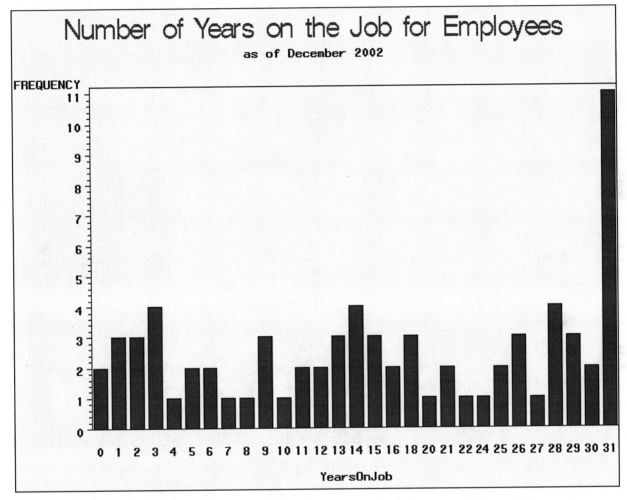

Notice that some of the numbers are missing in the chart. For example, the numbers 17 and 19 do not
appear because no one in the data set has 17 or 19 years on the job.

3. Produce a bar chart that shows the average salary of the employees in each department. Use formats to display the salary figures and include a blue title.

```
    title color=blue 'Average Salary by Department';
    vbar dept / sumvar=salary
                type=mean;
    format salary dollar8.;
run;
quit;
```

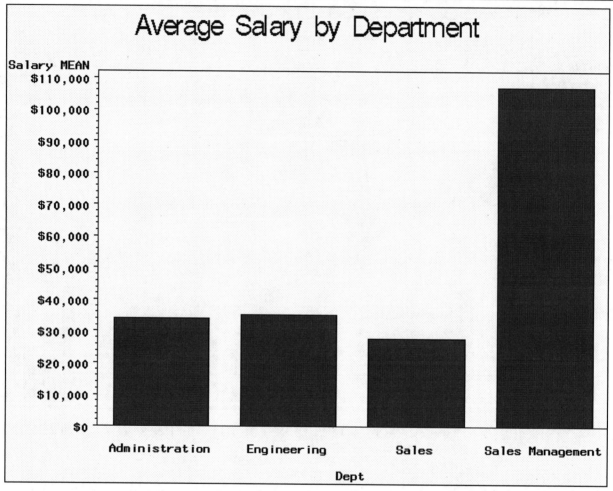

The average Sales Management salaries are much higher than the other departments.

 **Exercises**

1. **Creating Bar Charts and Pie Charts**

   All of these exercises use the **univ.employees** data set.

   a. Assign the **univ** libref to the permanent SAS library where the data sets for this course are stored.

   b. Using the GCHART procedure, generate a vertical bar chart that displays the number of employees for each manager.

   c. Using the GCHART procedure, generate a pie chart that displays the number of employees for each manager.

   d. Using the GCHART procedure, generate a vertical bar chart that displays the average bonus given by each manager.

   e. When using the GCHART procedure to generate a bar chart of a numeric variable, you can use the MIDPOINTS = option to specify how the data is binned in the chart. Use the VBAR statement shown below in a PROC GCHART step to generate a bar chart of the variable **bonus**.

   ```
   vbar bonus / midpoints=(0 2000 4000 6000 8000 10000);
   ```

The GPLOT Procedure

You can use the GPLOT procedure to plot one variable against another within a set of coordinate axes.

General form of a PROC GPLOT step:

PROC GPLOT DATA=*SAS-data-set*;
　　　PLOT *vertical-variable*horizontal-variable </options>*;
RUN;
QUIT;

24

The GPLOT Procedure

Produce a plot of salary versus bonus for each employee.

```
proc gplot data=univ.employees;
   plot Salary*Bonus;
   title 'Relationship of Salary and Bonus';
run;
```

25   c02s1d3.sas

The GPLOT Procedure

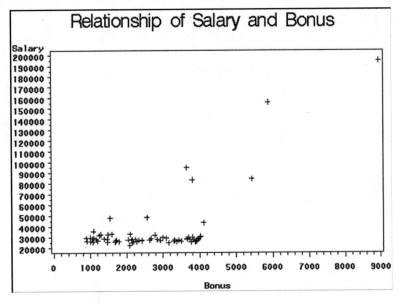

26

SYMBOL Statement

You can use the SYMBOL statement to do the following:

- define plotting symbols
- draw lines through the data points
- specify the color of the plotting symbols and lines

General form of the SYMBOL statement:

> **SYMBOL**n options;

The value of n can range from 1 to 255.

If n is omitted, the default is 1.

27

SYMBOL Statement

SYMBOL statements are global and additive.

global	After being defined, the statements remain in effect until changed or until the end of the SAS session.
additive	Specifying the value of one option does not affect the values of other options.

28

SYMBOL Statement Options

You can specify the plotting symbol you want with the VALUE= option in the SYMBOL statement:

VALUE=symbol | **V=**symbol

Selected symbol values are shown below:

PLUS (default)	DIAMOND
STAR	TRIANGLE
SQUARE	NONE (no plotting symbol)

29

SYMBOL Statement Options

You can use the I= option in the SYMBOL statement to draw lines between the data points.

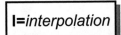

I=_interpolation_

Selected _interpolation_ values:

JOIN	joins the points with straight lines.
SPLINE	joins the points with a smooth line.
NEEDLE	draws vertical lines from the points to the horizontal axes.
R	overlays a simple linear regression line on the plot.

30

SYMBOL Statement Options

Use a star as the plotting symbol and superimpose a regression line on the plot.

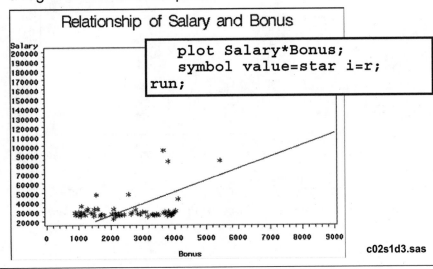

```
plot Salary*Bonus;
symbol value=star i=r;
run;
```

c02s1d3.sas

31

Producing Scatter Plots

c02s1d3.sas

You are interested in the relationship between the salaries and bonuses.

1. Generate a scatter plot of the two variables **salary** and **bonus** and include a red title.

```
proc gplot data=univ.employees;
   plot salary*bonus;
   title color=red 'Relationship of Salary and Bonus';
run;
```

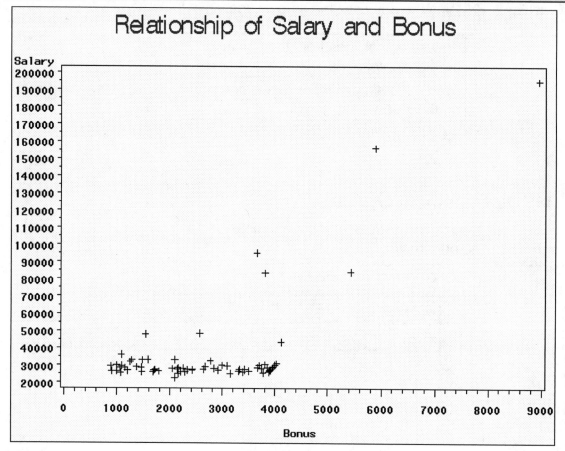

At the very highest salaries, employees receive higher bonuses. At the lower end of the salary scale, there does not appear to be much of a relationship between salary and bonus.

2. Generate another scatter plot of the two variables with some additional options:

   a. Use a star as the symbol for the points on the plot.

   b. Superimpose a regression line on the plot.

   c. Specify a font to be used for the title and keep the title red.

   d. Format both the salaries and the bonuses.

```
   plot salary*bonus;
   symbol value=star i=r;
   title font=brush color=red 'Relationship of Salary and Bonus';
   format salary dollar8. bonus dollar6.;
run;

quit;
```

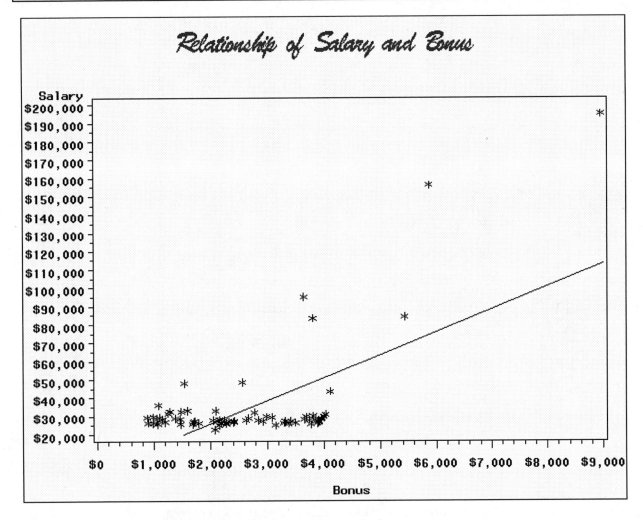

You can see the results of the additional options in the graph above.

Additional SYMBOL Statement Options

You can enhance the appearance of the plots with the following selected options:

WIDTH=width **W=**width	specifies the thickness of the line.
COLOR=color **C=**color	specifies the color of the line and plot symbols.

33

Additional SYMBOL Statement Options

Show the line in green with triple thickness.

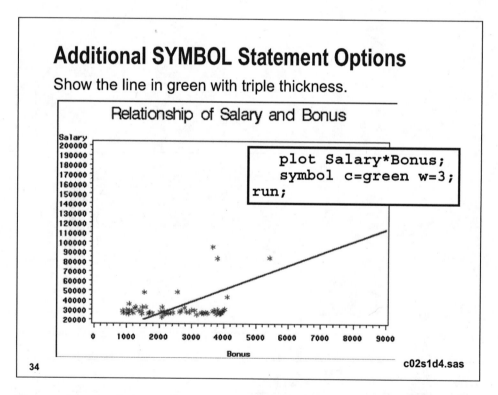

```
plot Salary*Bonus;
  symbol c=green w=3;
run;
```

34   c02s1d4.sas

The previous symbol statement options (V=STAR and I=R) remain in effect because new values for these options have not been assigned.

Canceling SYMBOL Statements

You can cancel a SYMBOL statement by submitting
a null SYMBOL statement.

```
symbol1;
```

To cancel all SYMBOL statements, submit the following
statement:

```
goptions reset=symbol;
```

35

Controlling the Axis Appearance

You can modify the appearance of the axes that
PROC GPLOT produces with the following:

- PLOT statement options
- the LABEL statement
- the FORMAT statement

36

PLOT Statement Options

You can use PLOT statement options to control the scaling and color of the axes, and the color of the axis text.

Selected PLOT statement options for axis control:

HAXIS=_values_	scales the horizontal axis.
VAXIS=_values_	scales the vertical axis.
CAXIS=_color_	specifies the color of both axes.
CTEXT=_color_	specifies the color of the text on both axes.

37

PLOT Statement Options

Define the scale on the vertical axis and display the axis text in blue.

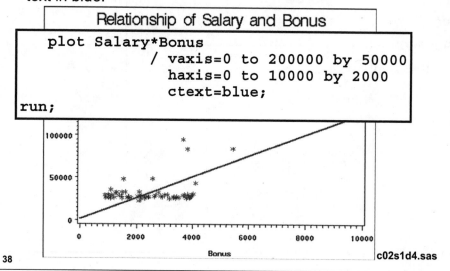

```
plot Salary*Bonus
            / vaxis=0 to 200000 by 50000
              haxis=0 to 10000 by 2000
              ctext=blue;
run;
```

38   c02s1d4.sas

LABEL Statement

Place labels on the axes.

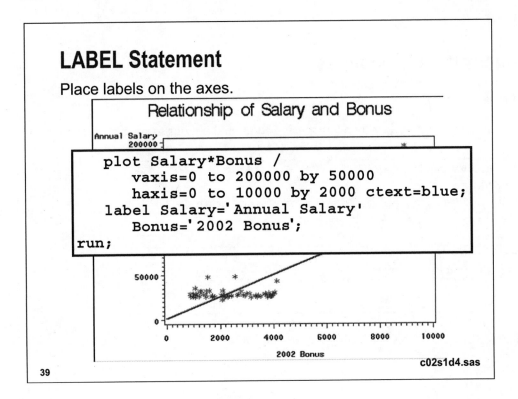

```
   plot Salary*Bonus /
      vaxis=0 to 200000 by 50000
      haxis=0 to 10000 by 2000 ctext=blue;
   label Salary='Annual Salary'
      Bonus='2002 Bonus';
run;
```

c02s1d4.sas

39

Using Scatter Plot Options

c02s1d4.sas

1. Generate another scatter plot of **salary** by **bonus** using additional options to specify green plotting symbols and a wider line width.

```
proc gplot data=univ.employees;
   plot salary*bonus;
   title color=red 'Relationship of Salary and Bonus';
   symbol c=green w=3;
run;
```

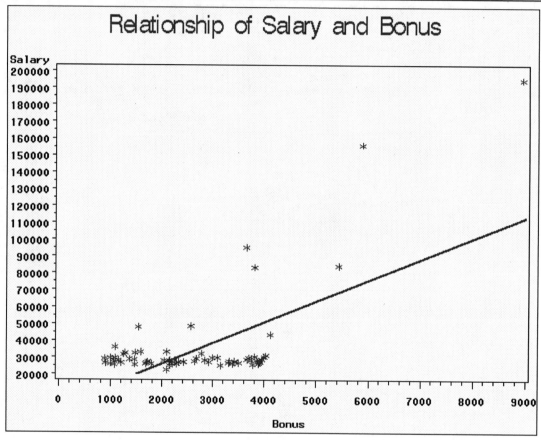

2. Generate the same scatter plot making use of additional options:

a. Specify values for the vertical and horizontal axes.

b. Make the axis labels blue.

c. Use labels instead of variable names on the axes.

d. Format the dollar and bonus amounts.

```
plot salary*bonus / vaxis=0 to 200000 by 50000
                    haxis=0 to 10000 by 2000
                    ctext=blue;
label salary='Annual Salary'
      Bonus='2002 Bonus';
format salary dollar8. bonus dollar6.;
run;

quit;
```

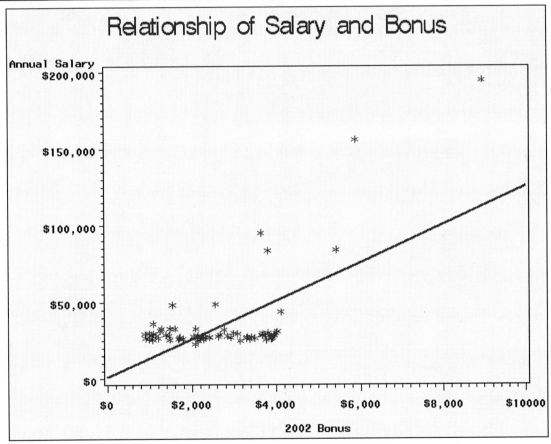

SAS/GRAPH Syntax

You can learn more about basic SAS/GRAPH syntax
by doing the following:

- take the self-paced training available

  http://www.sas.com/apps/elearning/elearning_courses.jsp?
  cat=SAS+Programming

- read the SAS/GRAPH documentation

  http://support.sas.com/documentation/onlinedoc/91pdf/
  sasdoc_91/graph_ref_6960.pdf

- use the SAS/GRAPH sample programs

  http://support.sas.com/techsup/sample/sample_graph.html

- take the SAS Color Graphics course

  http://support.sas.com/training/us/crs/grap9.html

41

Exercises

2. Generating a Scatter Plot

Generate a scatter plot of salary versus years on the job. Experiment with various options in the GPLOT procedure including titles, symbols, colors, formats, and labels.

2.2   Device Drivers (Self-Study)

Objective

- Explain the use of device drivers in SAS/GRAPH.

44

What Is a Device Driver?

To produce graphics output, SAS/GRAPH software uses a device driver. Device drivers are the components of SAS/GRAPH software that translate the device-independent output from SAS/GRAPH procedures into the appropriate command to produce graphics output.

Device drivers determine such items as the following:

- dimensions and orientation
- default text size
- colors
- hardware fonts

45

What Is a Device Driver?

SAS device drivers fall into the following categories:
- Client device drivers
  - ActiveX and JAVA drivers
- Non-client (or server-side) device drivers
  - Export
  - Camera
  - Graphics File Formats (such as GIF and JPG)

46

Selecting a Device Driver

To select a device driver, use the GOPTIONS statement.

General form of the GOPTIONS statement with the DEVICE option:

GOPTIONS DEVICE|DEV=<device-driver-name>;

Usually SAS/GRAPH automatically selects a device driver for you and you are not required to explicitly specify one. If you use the GRAPH window to display graphics output, SAS/GRAPH selects a device driver that is appropriate for your device.

47

Selecting a Device Driver

Examples:

Graphics Device	GOPTIONS Statement
Portable Document	goptions dev=PDF;
PostScript Driver	goptions dev=PSL;
Windows Metafile Driver	goptions dev=WMF;
GIF Driver	goptions dev=GIF;
Windows Color Printer	goptions dev=WINPRTC;
Windows Gray Scale Printer	goptions dev=WINPRTG;
UNIX Color Printer	goptions dev=SASPRTC;

48

Client Device Drivers

- ACTIVEX- and JAVA-related drivers
  - ACTIVEX interactive driver
  - JAVA interactive driver
  - ACTXIMG driver – noninteractive driver that creates graphs similar in appearance to the ActiveX interactive driver
  - JAVAIMG driver – noninteractive driver that creates graphs similar in appearance to the Java interactive driver

For more information about ACTIVEX and JAVA device drivers, consult these Technical Support documents:
http://support.sas.com/techsup/technote/ts602.html
http://support.sas.com/techsup/technote/ts601.html

49

Using ACTIVEX and JAVA Drivers

- The ACTIVEX, JAVA, ACTXIMG, and JAVAIMG drivers can only be used with the Output Delivery System (ODS).

- The ACTIVEX and JAVA drivers create graphs as ActiveX controls and Java applets. These graphs can be manipulated by the user.

- The ACTXIMG and JAVAIMG drivers create graphs that are identical in appearance to those produced by the ACTIVEX and JAVA drivers, but the graphs are static images and cannot be manipulated by the user.

50

Client Device Drivers: ACTXIMG Example

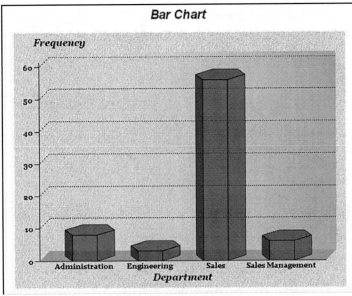

51

Printing Your Graphs

If your hardcopy device is a printer, select a WINPRTx driver under Windows or a SASPRTx driver under UNIX.

52

Non-Client Device Drivers

If you produce output that is to be exported to other software applications or files, select one of the drivers shown below:

- JPEG
- GIF
- PNG
- EMF
- WMF
- CGM

- PS
- EPSI
- PDF
- BMP
- TIFFB (monochrome)
- TIFFP (color)

For more information about exporting graphic files to Microsoft Office, consult this Technical Support document: http://support.sas.com/techsup/technote/ts674/ts674.pdf

53

Non-Client Device Drivers: GIF Example

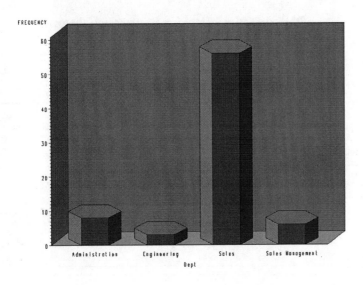

54

Enhancing SAS/GRAPH Output

When you want to enhance SAS/GRAPH output, your preferred method of enhancement depends on the device driver you use.

- If you use the client drivers (ACTIVEX, JAVA, ACTXIMG, JAVAIMG), then you can change the style elements or properties defined in the ODS style templates (such as WATERCOLOR, BANKER, ASTRONOMY, and GEARS). Any changes that you make inside the SAS/GRAPH syntax override the style template presentation elements.

- If you use the non-client drivers (such as GIF, JPG, and WINPRTC), then you can change the presentation characteristics of the output with SAS/GRAPH syntax.

55

2.3 Exercise Solutions

1. **Creating Bar Charts and Pie Charts**

   a. Assuming that the data sets are stored in the current working directory, assign the **univ** libref using the following LIBNAME statement:

   ```
   libname univ '.';
   ```

   Check the log to be sure that the libref has been successfully assigned.

   ```
   1    libname univ '.';
   NOTE: Libref UNIV was successfully assigned as follows:
         Engine:        V9
         Physical Name: C:\Workshop\winsas\HECPES
   ```

   b. Using the GCHART procedure, generate a vertical bar chart that displays the number of employees for each manager.

   ```
   proc gchart data=univ.employees;
      vbar manager;
   run;
   ```

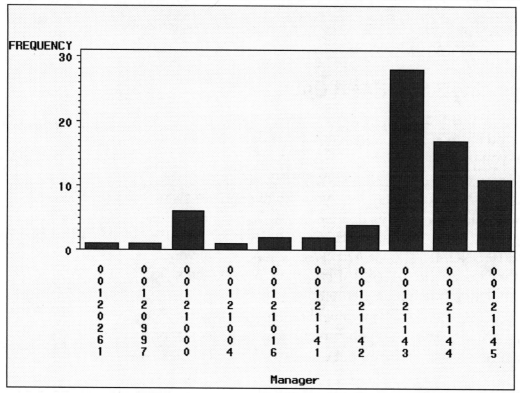

   Manager 00121143 has the most employees, with almost 30. Some managers have only one employee.

c. Using the GCHART procedure, generate a pie chart that displays the number of employees for each manager.

```
proc gchart data=univ.employees;
   pie manager;
run;
```

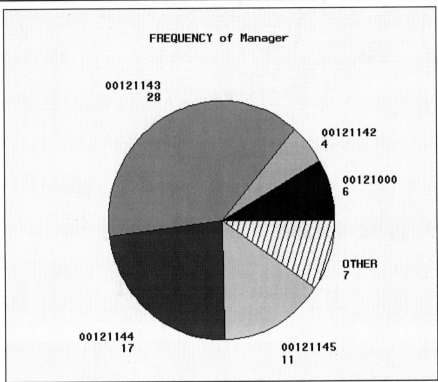

Note that the pie chart groups some managers into a category called OTHER. This will occur when any individual slice of the pie will represent 4% or less of the total. You can override this behavior with the OTHER = option in the PIE statement.

d. Using the GCHART procedure, generate a vertical bar chart that displays the average bonus given by each manager.

```
proc gchart data=univ.employees;
   vbar manager / sumvar=bonus
                  type=mean;
run;
```

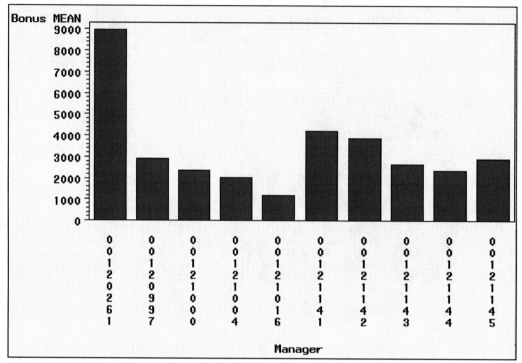

Manager 00120261 has the highest average Bonus, but recall that this manager had only one employee.

e. Use the MIDPOINTS = option in the VBAR statement to control how the data is binned in a vertical chart displaying the bonuses.

```
proc gchart data=univ.employees;
   vbar bonus / midpoints=(0 2000 4000 6000 8000 10000);
run;
```

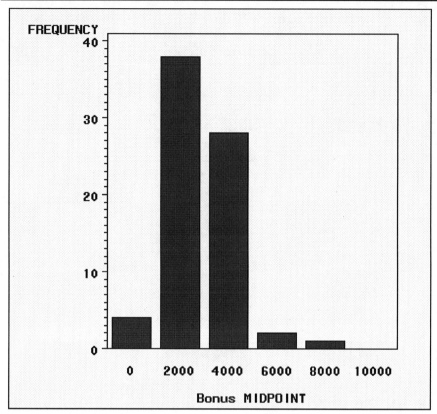

More employees received bonuses in the range from $1000 to $3000 than any other range.

2. Generating a Scatter Plot

Generate a scatter plot of salary versus years on the job. The program shown uses some of the options available in the GPLOT procedure, you may have chosen others.

```
proc gplot data=univ.employees;
   plot salary*yearsonjob;
   title color=red 'Relationship of Salary and Years on the Job';
   format salary dollar8.;
   label salary = 'Annual Salary' YearsOnJob = 'Years on the Job';
run;
quit;
```

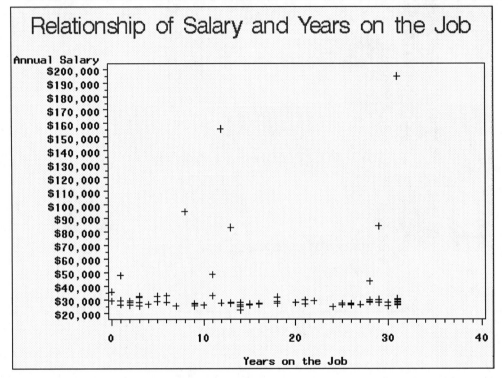

There does not appear to be a relationship between the number of years on the job and the salary of the individual.

Chapter 3   Modifying SAS Data Sets

3.1   Creating a SAS Data Set 3-3

3.2   Creating a New Variable 3-15

3.3   Using Conditional Logic to Create a New Variable 3-31

3.4   Using a Simple DO Loop to Process Data..3-47

3.5   SAS Array Processing..3-57

3.6   Subsetting Data Rows..3-70

3.7   Solutions to Exercises 3-82

3.1 Creating a SAS Data Set

Objectives

- Create a SAS data set using another SAS data set as input.
- Read and create temporary and permanent SAS data sets.
- Select variables to store in a SAS data set.

3

Reading a SAS Data Set

In order to create a SAS data set using a SAS data set as input, you must do the following:

- start a DATA step and name the SAS data set being created (**DATA statement**)
- identify the input SAS data set (**SET statement**)

4

The INFILE and INPUT statements are used to read external files. The SET statement is used to read SAS data sets.

Reading a SAS Data Set

General form of a DATA step:

```
DATA SAS-data-set ;
    SET SAS-data-set ;
            <additional SAS statements>
RUN;
```

Example:

```
data univ.customerorders;
   set work.customerorders;
run;
```

5

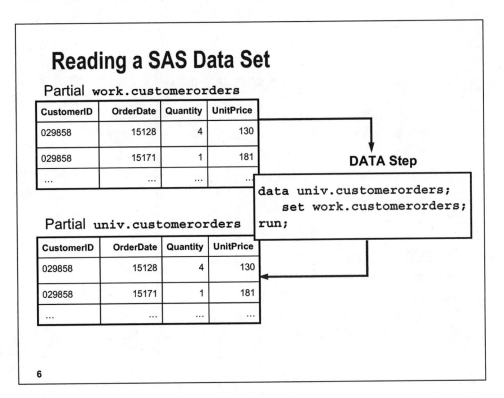

Reading a SAS Data Set

Partial `work.customerorders`

CustomerID	OrderDate	Quantity	UnitPrice
029858	15128	4	130
029858	15171	1	181
...	...	...	...

DATA Step

```
data univ.customerorders;
    set work.customerorders;
run;
```

Partial `univ.customerorders`

CustomerID	OrderDate	Quantity	UnitPrice
029858	15128	4	130
029858	15171	1	181
...	...	...	...

6

The DATA statement serves as the beginning of the DATA step and identifies `univ.customerorders` as the output data set. The SET statement instructs the DATA step to read from `work.customerorders`.

 Any data set not in the WORK library is a permanent SAS data set and is available for use after the current SAS session ends.

Reading a SAS Data Set

By default, the SET statement reads all of the

- observations
- variables

from the input SAS data set.

7

Selecting Variables to Store in a SAS Data Set

You can use a DROP= or KEEP= data set option in a
DATA statement to control which variables are written
to the new SAS data set.

General form of the DROP= and KEEP= data set options:

> *SAS-data-set*(**DROP=***variables*)
> or
> *SAS-data-set*(**KEEP=***variables*)

8

Use the DROP= data set option to specify the variables that are **not** to be written to the output data set.
Use the KEEP= data set option to specify the variables that are to be written to the output data set.

 As a timesaver, use the option that requires the least amount of typing. Never use both options
with one data set; they are mutually exclusive.

Selecting Variables to Store in a SAS Data Set

General form of the DROP= and KEEP= data set options
in a DATA statement:

DATA *output-SAS-data-set*(KEEP=*variables*);
    SET *input-SAS-data-set*;
RUN;

9

Selecting Variables to Store in a SAS Data Set

`work.customerorders`

CustomerID	OrderDate	OrderID	ProductID	Quantity	UnitPrice
029858	15128	1239347234	230100600005	4	130
029858	15171	1239686972	240800100020	1	122
. . .	. . .	. . .	. . .	. . .	. . .

```
data univ.productorders(keep= ProductID Quantity
                               UnitPrice);
   set work.customerorders;
run;
```

`univ.productorders`

ProductID	Quantity	UnitPrice
230100600005	4	130
240800100020	1	122
...	...	...

10

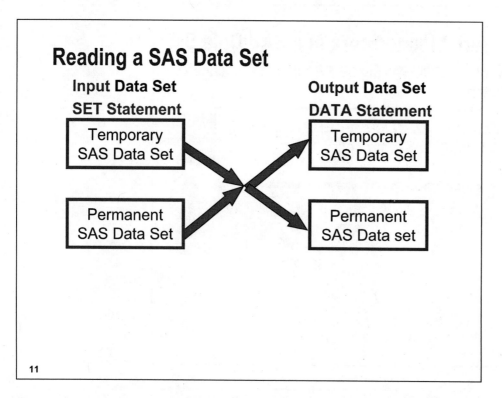

Reading a SAS Data Set

Input Data Set
SET Statement

Output Data Set
DATA Statement

Temporary SAS Data Set

Permanent SAS Data Set

Temporary SAS Data Set

Permanent SAS Data set

11

You can use the DATA step to read and write any combination of temporary and permanent SAS data sets.

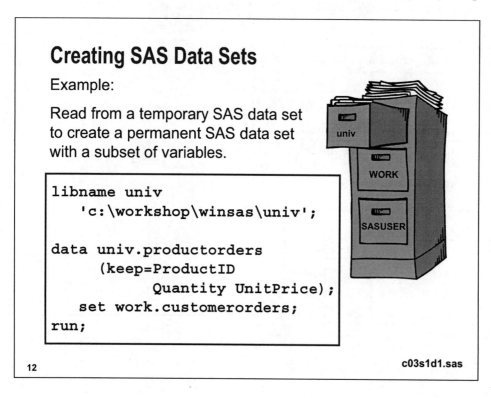

Creating SAS Data Sets

Example:

Read from a temporary SAS data set to create a permanent SAS data set with a subset of variables.

```
libname univ
    'c:\workshop\winsas\univ';

data univ.productorders
    (keep=ProductID
          Quantity UnitPrice);
    set work.customerorders;
run;
```

univ

WORK

SASUSER

12   c03s1d1.sas

Creating a New SAS Data Set from an Existing SAS Data Set

c03s1d1.sas

- Use the LIBNAME statement to assign the **univ** libref to the appropriate SAS data library.
- Use the CONTENTS procedure to examine the contents of the **univ** data library.
- Use the CONTENTS procedure to examine the descriptor portion of **work.customerorders** data set.
- Use the DATA step to read from a temporary SAS data set and create a new permanent SAS data set.
- Use the CONTENTS procedure to examine the descriptor portion of the new SAS data set.
- Use the DATA step to read from a SAS data set and create a new SAS data set with selected variables.
- Use the CONTENTS procedure to examine the descriptor portion of the new SAS data set.

Assigning a Libref

Assign the **univ** libref to the permanent SAS library where the data sets for this course are stored.

```
libname univ '.';
```

SAS Log

```
1    libname univ '.';
NOTE: Libref UNIV was successfully assigned as follows:
      Engine:        V9
      Physical Name: c:\workshop\winsas\univ
```

Examining Contents of a SAS Data Library

1. Use PROC CONTENTS to examine the contents of the **univ** SAS data library. Use the _ALL_ keyword for a list of data sets and the NODS option to suppress printing of the descriptor portion of each data set.

```
proc contents data=univ._all_ nods;
run;
```

Partial SAS Output

```
                                           The CONTENTS Procedure

                              Directory

                   Libref        UNIV
                   Engine        V9
                   Physical Name C:\Workshop\winsas\univ
                   File Name     C:\Workshop\winsas\univ


                                       Member    File
                # Name                 Type      Size  Last Modified

                1 CUSTOMERORDERS       DATA      17408 22Mar07:16:37:10
                2 CUSTOMERS            DATA      82944 23Mar07:16:53:28
                3 DAILYSALES2001       DATA      66560 13Apr04:14:27:30
```

2. PROC CONTENTS can also display the descriptor portion of a SAS data set.

```
proc contents data=work.customerorders;
   title 'Customer Order Data';
run;
```

The descriptor portion of a SAS data set contains general information about a SAS data set and variable attributes.

Partial SAS Output

```
                              Customer Order Data

                   Alphabetic List of Variables and Attributes

                   #    Variable     Type     Len

                   1    CustomerID   Char      6
                   2    OrderDate    Num       8
                   3    OrderID      Char     10
                   4    ProductID    Char     12
                   5    Quantity     Num       8
                   6    UnitPrice    Num       8
```

Turning a Temporary SAS Data Set into a Permanent SAS Data Set

3. Read all of the observations and variables from a temporary SAS data set.

```
data univ.customerorders;
   set work.customerorders;
run;
```

SAS Log

```
53   data univ.customerorders;
54      set work.customerorders;
55   run;

NOTE: There were 201 observations read from the data set WORK.CUSTOMERORDERS.
NOTE: The data set UNIV.CUSTOMERORDERS has 201 observations and 6 variables.
NOTE: DATA statement used (Total process time):
      real time           0.43 seconds cpu time           0.02 seconds
```

4. Use PROC CONTENTS to examine the descriptor portion of the new data set.

```
proc contents data=univ.customerorders;
   title 'Customer Order Data';
run;
```

Partial SAS Output

```
                        Customer Order Data

            Alphabetic List of Variables and Attributes

                #    Variable      Type    Len

                1    CustomerID    Char      6
                2    OrderDate     Num       8
                3    OrderID       Char     10
                4    ProductID     Char     12
                5    Quantity      Num       8
                6    UnitPrice     Num       8
```

Creating a New SAS Data Set with Selected Variables

5. Read all of the observations and variables from a temporary SAS data set. Create a new SAS data set, keeping only the desired variables.

```
data univ.productorders (keep=ProductID Quantity UnitPrice);
   set work.customerorders;
run;
```

SAS Log

```
53  data univ.productorders (keep=ProductID Quantity UnitPrice);
54     set work.customerorders;
55  run;

NOTE: There were 201 observations read from the data set WORK.CUSTOMERORDERS.
NOTE: The data set UNIV.CUSTOMERDATA has 201 observations and 3 variables.
NOTE: DATA statement used (Total process time):
      real time           0.43 seconds cpu time          0.02 seconds
```

   Instead of using the KEEP=data set option in the DATA statement, you can use the DROP= data set option. The syntax for this example is as follows:

```
data univ.productorders (drop = OrderDate OrderID CustomerID);
   set work.customerorders;
run;
```

6. Examine the descriptor portion of the new SAS data set.

```
title;
proc contents data=univ.productorders;
run;
```

Partial SAS Output

```
            Alphabetic List of Variables and Attributes

             #    Variable     Type    Len

             1    ProductID    Char     12
             2    Quantity     Num       8
             3    UnitPrice    Num       8
```

 **Exercises**

1. **Using the DATA Step to Create a SAS Data Set**

    a. Use the **univ.dailysales2001** data set to create a new data set named **work.sales2001** with the following characteristic:

        *   **work.sales2001** should only contain the variables **EmployeeID**, **EmployeeGroup**, **EmployeeManager**, **OrderDate**, and **SaleAmount**.

    b. Use PROC PRINT to produce a list report of **work.sales2001**.

        Partial SAS Output

```
                                    The SAS System

            Employee                            Employee                   Sale
     Obs      ID       EmployeeGroup            Manager    OrderDate       Amount

      1     00121091   Running - Jogging        00121143   03-JAN-01        34.50
      2     00121042   Clothes                  00121144   05-JAN-01        53.00
      3     00121105   Team Sports              00121143   07-JAN-01        18.80
      4     00121060   Shoes                    00121143   11-JAN-01       141.20
      5     00121044   Clothes                  00121144   13-JAN-01        16.00
      6     00121073   Outdoors                 00121145   16-JAN-01       984.50
      7     00121064   Outdoors                 00121145   19-JAN-01       220.00
      8     00121039   Clothes                  00121144   20-JAN-01       112.00
      9     00121069   Outdoors                 00121145   24-JAN-01       259.60
     10     00121039   Clothes                  00121144   25-JAN-01        78.80
     11     00121057   Shoes                    00121143   25-JAN-01       144.50
     12     00121056   Shoes                    00121143   25-JAN-01       141.20
     13     00121044   Clothes                  00121144   25-JAN-01       142.30
     14     00121037   Clothes                  00121144   26-JAN-01        18.20
     15     00121064   Outdoors                 00121145   27-JAN-01       470.80
     16     00121043   Clothes                  00121144   27-JAN-01        63.00
     17     00121068   Outdoors                 00121145   30-JAN-01        96.60
     18     00121020   Assorted Sports Articles 00121144   02-FEB-01       124.00
     19     00121044   Clothes                  00121144   04-FEB-01       134.00
     20     00121043   Clothes                  00121144   04-FEB-01       141.90
     21     00121043   Clothes                  00121144   05-FEB-01        29.40
     22     00121029   Children Sports          00121144   05-FEB-01        47.70
     23     00121042   Clothes                  00121144   06-FEB-01       106.80
     24     00121058   Shoes                    00121143   07-FEB-01       211.80
     25     00121061   Shoes                    00121143   08-FEB-01       141.70
     26     00121040   Clothes                  00121144   10-FEB-01       112.20
     27     00121106   Team Sports              00121143   11-FEB-01        46.59
     28     00121020   Assorted Sports Articles 00121144   13-FEB-01        39.30
     29     00121058   Shoes                    00121143   14-FEB-01        84.70
```

    c. Save the DATA step that created **work.sales2001** in a file named **ch3ex1.sas**.

3.2 Creating a New Variable

Objectives

- Explain the assignment statement.
- Explain SAS functions.
- Add a variable to an existing SAS data set.

16

Programming Objective

- Use the `customerorders` permanent data set as the input data set.
- Create a new data set that calculates the total sale price for each customer order.

17

The Assignment Statement

An *assignment statement* evaluates an expression and assigns the resulting value to a variable. Assignment statements are used in the DATA step.

General form of an assignment statement:

> *variable=expression;*

18

When a variable is created in an assignment statement, the type and length of the new variable is defined by the expression on the right side of the assignment statement.

Determine the Expression

The expression can be any valid combination of

- constants
- variables
- operators
- SAS functions
- parentheses

19

Constants can be of two types:

- numeric
- character

A *numeric constant* is any valid numerical value. A *character constant* is a string of text enclosed in quotation marks.

Operators and Parentheses

Symbol	Definition
+	Addition
-	Subtraction
*	Multiplication
/	Division
**	Exponentiation
( )	Grouping

20

Parentheses can be used as needed. Parentheses can be nested; in other words, one set of parentheses can be used within another set of parentheses.

Parentheses must be matched. Every left parenthesis should have a corresponding right parenthesis.

Creating a New Variable

Example: Create a new variable named **TotalSale** that is the **UnitPrice** multiplied by the **Quantity** purchased.

```
data univ.totalorders;
   set univ.customerorders;
   TotalSale = UnitPrice * Quantity;
run;
```

21

Using SAS Functions

A *SAS function* is a routine that returns a value that is determined from specified arguments.

General form of a SAS function:

> *function-name(argument1,argument2, . . .)*

22

Each argument is separated from other arguments by a comma. Most functions accept arguments that are

- constants
- variables
- expressions
- functions

The number of required arguments varies from function to function.

Using SAS Functions

SAS functions

- perform arithmetic operations
- compute statistics (for example, MEAN)
- manipulate SAS dates and process character values
- perform many other tasks

23

Selected Date Functions

YEAR(*SAS-date*)

> extracts the year from a SAS date
> and returns a four-digit value for year.

QTR(*SAS-date*)

> extracts the quarter from a SAS date
> and returns a number from 1 to 4.

MONTH(*SAS-date*)

> extracts the month from a SAS date
> and returns a number from 1 to 12.

INTNX('*interval* ', *start-from*, *increment*)

> advances a date, time, or datetime value
> by a given interval, and returns a date,
> time, or datetime value.

24

continued...

 An increment of 1 in the INTNX function advances forward to the beginning of the specified interval. An increment of 0 moves backward to the beginning of the interval.

Examples:

Variable: Date	Function	Returned Value
06JUL01	INTNX('month', *date*, 0)	01JUL01
06JUL01	INTNX('month', *date*, 1)	01AUG01

Recall that dates are stored as numeric values in SAS. Dates are represented in the table above using a SAS format.

Selected Date Functions

WEEKDAY(*SAS-date*)

extracts the day of the week from a
SAS date and returns a number from
1 to 7, where 1 represents Sunday,
and so on.

MDY(*month,day,year*)

uses the *month*, *day*, and *year* values
to return the corresponding SAS date
value.

TODAY()

obtains the date value from the system
clock.

25

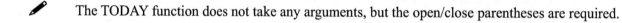

The TODAY function does not take any arguments, but the open/close parentheses are required.

Selected Character Functions

UPCASE(*argument*)
> converts all letters in an argument to uppercase.

SCAN(*argument, n <, dlm >*)
> returns a given word from a character expression.

FIND*(string,substring<,modifiers><,startpos>)*
> searches string for the first occurrence of the specified substring, and returns the position of that substring.

26   *continued...*

Example:

Variable Name	Variable Value	Function	Returned Value
Address2	Cary, NC, 27513	SCAN(address2, 2, ',')	NC
Jobtitle	Security Administration Manager	FIND(jobtitle, 'Manager')	25
	Sales Manager		7

     Character comparisons are case sensitive.

Selected Character Functions

SUBSTR(*argument, position, <, n>*)

   extracts or replaces specific characters
   in a character string. Placement of this
   function in a statement determines
   whether the string is replaced or extracted.

COMPRESS(*source <, characters to remove>*)

   removes specific characters from
   a character string.

27

When the SUBSTR function is used on the right side of an expression, it extracts a character string from the source. For example, the following assignment statements used in a DATA step creates a new variable that contains the name prefix:

```
Name='Miss Jane Smith';
NamePrefix=substr(Name, 1, 4);
/* The value of NamePrefix is Miss */
```

When the SUBSTR function is used on the left side of an expression, it specifies a character string to substitute into the source. For example, the following assignment statements used in a DATA step can be used to replace the prefix Miss with the prefix Ms.

```
name='Miss Jane Smith';
substr(Name, 1, 4)='Ms.';
/* The value of Name is Ms.  Jane Smith */
```

Selected Descriptive Statistics Functions

SUM(*argument, argument,. . .*)
> returns the sum of the arguments.

MEAN(*argument, argument,. . .*)
> returns the average of the arguments.

Example:

```
Quarter1=sum(mon1sales,mon2sales,mon3sales);
```

28

The SUM and MEAN functions ignore missing values.

Creating a New Variable with the Assignment Statement

c03s2d1.sas

Create a variable that indicates the total amount of each sale in the **univ.customerorders** data set.

- Create a permanent SAS data set.
- Use an assignment statement to create a new variable and assign its values.
- Use the PRINT procedure to create an enhanced list report.

1. Browse the descriptor portion and data portion of the **univ.customerorders** data set.

```
proc contents data=univ.customerorders;
run;
proc print data=univ.customerorders;
run;
```

Partial PROC CONTENTS Output

```
              Alphabetic List of Variables and Attributes

              #      Variable      Type      Len

              1      CustomerID    Char       6
              2      OrderDate     Num        8
              3      OrderID       Char      10
              4      ProductID     Char      12
              5      Quantity      Num        8
              6      UnitPrice     Num        8
```

Partial PROC PRINT Output

```
                            The SAS System

         Customer   Order                                              Unit
  Obs       ID      Date      OrderID      ProductID       Quantity   Price

    1     029858   15128   1239347234   230100600005          4        130
    2     029858   15171   1239686972   240800100020          1        122
    3     029858   15171   1239686972   240800100036          1        468
    4     029858   15171   1239686972   240800200009          1         87
    5     029858   15226   1240124979   220200100116          1        181
    6     029858   15265   1240437628   220200100179          1        135
```

2. Use a DATA step to create a permanent SAS data set named **univ.totalorders** from an existing SAS data set named **univ.customerorders**. Add an assignment statement to create a variable named **TotalSale**. Drop the **OrderDate**, **OrderID**, and **ProductID** variables from the new data set.

```
data univ.totalorders (drop= OrderDate OrderID ProductID);
   set univ.customerorders;
   TotalSale=UnitPrice*Quantity;
run;
```

Submit the program for execution and browse the messages in the SAS log.

The log

- does not contain any warnings or error messages
- indicates that the data set **univ.totalorders** was created with 201 observations and 4 variables.

Partial SAS Log

```
25    data univ.totalorders;
26       set univ.customerorders;
27       TotalSale=UnitPrice*Quantity;
28    run;

NOTE: Missing values were generated as a result of performing an operation on missing values.
      Each place is given by: (Number of times) at (Line):(Column).
      2 at 27:23
NOTE: There were 201 observations read from the data set UNIV.CUSTOMERORDERS.
NOTE: The data set UNIV.TOTALORDERS has 201 observations and 4 variables.
NOTE: DATA statement used (Total process time):
      real time           0.31 seconds
      cpu time            0.12 seconds
```

3. Use the PRINT procedure to generate a list report that indicates the total sales amounts for each order placed and an overall total for all sales. Add appropriate FORMAT and LABEL statements.

```
title 'Total Sales Report';
proc print data=univ.totalorders noobs label;
   var CustomerID Quantity UnitPrice TotalSale;
   format UnitPrice TotalSale dollar11.;
   label CustomerId = 'Customer ID'
         Quantity = 'Total Units Sold'
         UnitPrice = 'Price Per Unit'
         TotalSale = 'Total Sale';
run;
```

Partial SAS Output

```
                         Total Sales Report

                        Total
             Customer    Units    Price Per
               ID        Sold       Unit      Total Sale

             029858        4        $130         $520
             029858        1        $122         $122
             029858        1        $468         $468
             029858        1         $87          $87
             029858        1        $181         $181
             029858        1        $135         $135
             029858        1         $23          $23
             030643        2         $19          $38
             030643        2         $25          $50
             031116        2        $132         $264
             031116        2         $84         $168
             032096        1         $63          $63
```

 **Exercises**

2. **Creating New Variables**

    a. Recall the DATA step that created **work.sales2001**. If necessary, open the program
        ch3ex1.sas or **bkup31.sas** in the Editor Window.

    ```
    data work.sales2001(keep=EmployeeID EmployeeGroup EmployeeManager
                        OrderDate SaleAmount);
       set univ.dailysales2001;
    run;
    ```

    b. Modify the DATA step by creating two new variables.

        • **Commission** contains a 3% commission on each sale amount.

        • **SaleMonth** contains the month when the order was placed. This value needs to be in
          the form of JAN-01. To create this character variable, use the SCAN function to extract
          the three-letter abbreviation for month from the **OrderDate** variable.

    c. Run the DATA step and view the log to ensure that **work.sales2001** includes the two new
        variables. View the descriptor portion of the data set.

        Partial SAS Output

        -----Alphabetic List of Variables and Attributes-----

#	Variable	Type	Len	Pos	Format	Label
6	Commission	Num	8	8		
2	EmployeeGroup	Char	40	24	$25.	Employee Group
1	EmployeeID	Char	8	16		Employee ID
3	EmployeeManager	Char	8	64		Employee Manager ID
4	OrderDate	Char	9	72		
5	SaleAmount	Num	8	0		
7	SaleMonth	Char	200	81		

d. Use the PRINT procedure to generate the list report displayed below. Add FORMAT and LABEL statements, as needed.

Partial SAS Output

```
                     2001 Sales and Salaries for Sales Teams

       Date
        of      Manager    Employee                                    Sales
       Order      ID       Group                   Commission         Revenue

     05-DEC-01  00121144   Clothes                    $3.23           $107.60
     06-DEC-01  00121145   Outdoors                   $3.56           $118.60
     06-DEC-01  00121143   Team Sports                $0.72            $23.98
     06-DEC-01  00121144   Assorted Sports Articles   $7.55           $251.80
     06-DEC-01  00121143   Shoes                     $10.20           $340.00
     09-DEC-01  00121144   Clothes                    $5.86           $195.40
     11-DEC-01  00121144   Clothes                   $11.50           $383.20
     11-DEC-01  00121144   Clothes                    $4.84           $161.20
     13-DEC-01  00121144   Clothes                   $31.43         $1,047.60
     14-DEC-01  00121144   Clothes                    $0.79            $26.40
     15-DEC-01  00121144   Assorted Sports Articles   $4.75           $158.40
     17-DEC-01  00121143   Golf                      $19.30           $643.20
     17-DEC-01  00121145   Outdoors                   $2.55            $85.10
     20-DEC-01  00121144   Clothes                    $1.63            $54.40
     22-DEC-01  00121144   Clothes                    $6.37           $212.40
     22-DEC-01  00121143   Shoes                      $8.69           $289.60
     23-DEC-01  00121144   Children Sports            $1.23            $41.00
```

e. Use the GCHART procedure to generate the summary report displayed below.

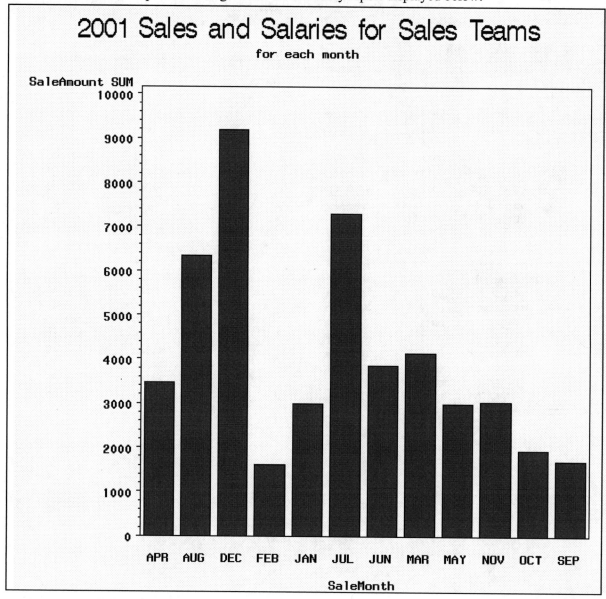

f. Save your work as **ch3ex2.sas**.

3.3 Using Conditional Logic to Create a New Variable

Objectives

- Explain conditional processing in SAS.
- Use conditional processing to create a new variable in a SAS data set.
- Control the length of character variables explicitly with the LENGTH statement.

32

The Programming Need

- Create a new variable named **Level** in the **univ.totalorders** data set.
- The value of **Level** is dependent upon the value of the variable **TotalSale**.

33

Conditional Statements

Conditional statements can create values for a new variable based on whether a condition is true or false.

General form of the IF-THEN and ELSE statements:

IF *expression* **THEN** *statement*;
ELSE IF *expression* **THEN** *statement*;
. . .

34

The conditional statements can only be used in the DATA step.

Only one statement (action) can follow the THEN statement.

Determining the Condition

The condition can be specified as an expression that contains any valid combination of

- constants
- variables
- functions
- operators and/or parentheses.

35

Comparison Operators

Mnemonic	Symbol	Definition
EQ	=	equal to
NE	^=	not equal to
GT	>	greater than
LT	<	less than
GE	>=	greater than or equal to
LE	<=	less than or equal to
IN		equal to one of a list

36

Comparison Operators

Examples:

```
if TotalSales>25000 then ...;
```

```
if CustomerID='029858' then ...;
```

```
if UnitPrice=. then ...;
```

```
if RepName=' ' then ...;
```

```
if month(OrderDate)=1 then ...;
```

37

Comparison Operator

You can use the IN comparison operator to see
if a variable is equal to one of the values in a list.

Example:

```
if month(OrderDate) in (1,2,3)
then ...;
```

```
if CustomerID in ('030643', '031116')
then ...;
```

38

Logical Operators

Logical operators include the following:

AND   If both expressions are true, then the compound
      expression is true.

OR   If either expression is true, then the compound
      expression is true.

NOT   This operator can be combined with other
      operators to reverse the logic of a comparison.

39

The logic operators should be used to build complex conditions.

Logical Operators

Examples:

```
if RepName='Bradshaw' and TotalPrice > 500
   then ...;
if RepName='Bradshaw' or
   RepName='Conner' or
   RepName='Smith'
   then ...;
```

Character comparisons are case sensitive.

40

Determining the Action

When a condition is true, the action can include
the following:
- create a new variable
- modify an existing variable
- output the observation

41

Conditionally Executing Statements

```
data univ.totalorders;
   set univ.customerorders;
   TotalSale=UnitPrice*Quantity;
   if Quantity in (1,2) then Level='Level I';
   else if Quantity=3 then Level='Level II';
   else if Quantity ge 4 then Level='Level III';
   else Level='Miscoded';
run;
```

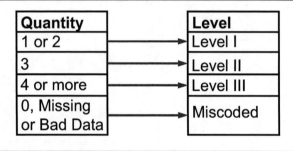

Quantity	Level
1 or 2	Level I
3	Level II
4 or more	Level III
0, Missing or Bad Data	Miscoded

42   c03s3d1.sas

Listing Output

Partial Output

```
Quantity     Level      Total Sale

   1        Level I        $20
   3        Level I        $234
   1        Level I        $50
   5        Level I        $560
   1        Level I        $12
   2        Level I        $84
   2        Level I        $46
```

Where are the Level II and Level III values?

43   ...

The LENGTH Statement

You can use the LENGTH statement to define the length of a variable explicitly.

General form of the LENGTH statement:

LENGTH *variable(s)* $ *length*;

Example:

```
length Level $ 9;
```

44

The LENGTH statement must occur prior to using the variable in an assignment statement in order to set the variable attributes correctly.

The LENGTH Statement

```
data univ.totalorders;
   set univ.customerorders;
   length Level $ 9;
   TotalSale=UnitPrice*Quantity;
   if Quantity in (1,2)then Level='Level I';
   else if Quantity=3 then Level='Level II';
   else if Quantity ge 4 then Level='Level III';
   else Level='Miscoded';
run;
```

c03s3d1.sas

45

Listing Output

Partial Output

```
Quantity        Level        Total Sale

   1          Level II            $20
   3          Level I            $234
   1          Level III           $50
   5          Level I            $560
   1          Level I             $12
   2          Level I             $84
   2          Level I             $46
```

What if more than one action needs to occur as a result of a condition?

46   ...

Business Need

Based on the quantity sold, assign both levels and discount awards for each order using the table below.

Quantity	Level	Discount Award
1 or 2	Level I	0
3	Level II	5%
4 or more	Level III	10%
0, bad, or missing data	Miscoded	0

47

Conditional Execution

You can use the DO and END statements to execute a group of statements based on a condition.

General form of the DO and END statements:

IF *expression* **THEN DO**;
   executable statements
END;
ELSE DO;
   executable statements
END;

48

Partial Code for Multiple Actions for a Condition

```
TotalSale=UnitPrice*Quantity;
if Quantity in (1,2) then do;
   Level='Level I';
   DiscountAward=0;
end;
else if Quantity=3 then do;
   Level= 'Level II';
   DiscountAward=TotalSale*.05;
end;
else if Quantity ge 4 then do;
   Level='Level III';
   DiscountAward=TotalSale*.10;
end;
else Level='Miscoded';
```

49

Creating a Variable Using Conditional Logic

c03s3d1.sas

- Use conditional logic to create a new variable.
- Use PROC PRINT to create a list report.
- Use DO and END statements with conditional logic to create multiple variables for each condition.
- Use PROC PRINT to create a list report.
- Use PROC GCHART to create a summary report.

Creating a Variable Using Conditional Logic

1. Create a new variable named **Level** based on the values of **Quantity**.

```
data univ.totalorders1 (drop= OrderDate OrderID ProductID);
   set univ.customerorders;
   TotalSale=UnitPrice*Quantity;
   if Quantity in (1,2) then Level='Level I';
   else if Quantity =3 then Level='Level II';
   else if Quantity >=4 then Level='Level III';
   else Level='Miscoded';
run;
```

2. Generate a list report that displays the customer orders.

```
title 'Total Sales';
proc print data=univ.totalorders1 noobs label ';
   var Quantity Level TotalSale;
   format TotalSale dollar11.;
   label TotalSale='Total Sale';
run;
```

Partial SAS Output

Total Sales		
Quantity	Level	Total Sale
4	Level I	$520
1	Level I	$122
1	Level I	$468
1	Level I	$87
1	Level I	$181
1	Level I	$135
1	Level I	$23
2	Level I	$38
2	Level I	$50
2	Level I	$264
2	Level I	$168
1	Level I	$63

3. There should be more than one level appearing in the **Level** column of the report. Examine the descriptor portion of **univ.totalorders1**. Notice that the length of the variable **Level** is set to 7, yet the longest value for the variable **Level** is Level III, which has a length of 9.

```
        Alphabetic List of Variables and Attributes

         #     Variable     Type     Len

         1     CustomerID   Char      6
         5     Level        Char      7
         2     Quantity     Num       8
         4     TotalSale    Num       8
         3     UnitPrice    Num       8
```

4. Add a LENGTH statement to the DATA step to set the length of **Level** to 9. Re-create the report by submitting the PRINT procedure.

```
data univ.totalorders2 (drop= OrderDate OrderID ProductID);
   set univ.customerorders;
   length Level $ 9;
   TotalSale=UnitPrice*Quantity;
   if Quantity in (1,2) then Level='Level I';
   else if Quantity =3 then Level='Level II';
   else if Quantity >=4 then Level='Level III';
   else Level='Miscoded';
run;
```

Partial SAS Output

```
                          Total Sales

                                      Total
        Quantity       Level           Sale

            4        Level III        $520
            1        Level I          $122
            1        Level I          $468
            1        Level I           $87
            1        Level I          $181
            1        Level I          $135
            1        Level I           $23
            2        Level I           $38
            2        Level I           $50
            2        Level I          $264
            2        Level I          $168
            1        Level I           $63
```

Creating Multiple Variables Using Conditional Logic

1. Calculate the discount awards for orders based on the **Quantity** and **Level** values displayed below.

Quantity	Level	Discountaward
1 or 2	Level I	0
3	Level II	5%
4 or more	Level III	10%
0, bad or missing data	Miscoded	0

2. Modify the DATA step that created **univ.totalorders2** to create **univ.totalorders3**.

  a. Use DO-END statements to create two variables, **Level** and **DiscountAward** that are based on the values of **Quantity**.

```
data univ.totalorders3 (drop=OrderDate OrderID ProductID);
   set univ.customerorders;
   length Level $ 9;
   TotalSale=UnitPrice*Quantity;
   if Quantity in (1,2)then do;
      Level='Level I';
      DiscountAward=0;
   end;
   else if Quantity=3 then do;
      Level='Level II';
      DiscountAward=TotalSale*.05;
   end;
   else if Quantity ge 4 then do;
      Level='Level III';
      DiscountAward=TotalSale*.10;
   end;
   else Level='Miscoded';
run;
```

  b. Use the PRINT procedure to create a report of the total discount amounts rewarded.

```
title 'Discount Award Program';
proc print data=univ.totalorders3 noobs label;
  var Level TotalSale DiscountAward;
  format TotalSale dollar11.;
  label TotalSale='Total Sales'
        DiscountAward='Total Award Value';
run;
```

Partial SAS Output

```
                       Discount Award Program

                                          Total
                                Total      Award
              Level             Sales      Value

              Level III         $520       52.00
              Level I           $122        0.00
              Level I           $468        0.00
              Level I            $87        0.00
              Level I           $181        0.00
              Level I           $135        0.00
              Level I            $23        0.00
              Level I            $38        0.00
              Level I            $50        0.00
              Level I           $264        0.00
              Level I           $168        0.00
              Level I            $63        0.00
              Level I            $54        0.00
              Level I            $17        0.00
              Level I           $116        0.00
              Level I           $104        0.00
              Level I           $126        0.00
              Level I           $118        0.00
```

c. Use the GCHART procedure to create a summary report of the total discount amounts within each level.

SAS Output

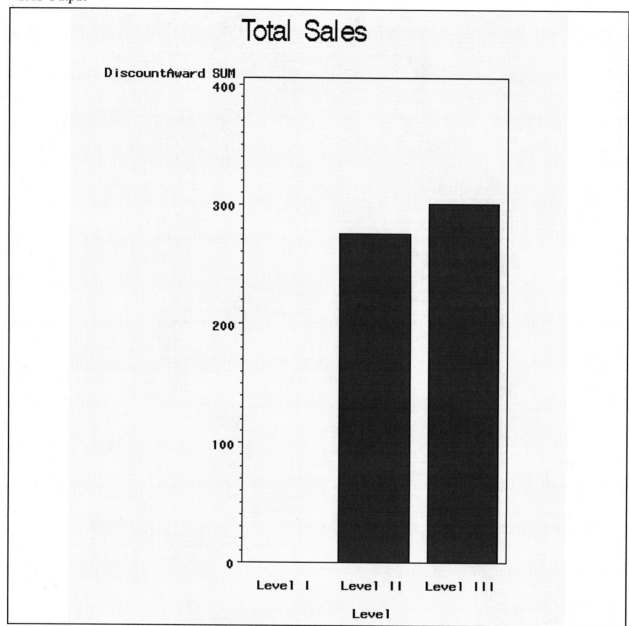

 **Exercises**

3. Modifying Values Using IF-THEN Logic

a. Open **ch3ex2.sas** or **bkup32.sas** into your Editor as a starting point for this exercise. Delete the PROC CONTENTS step so that you have the code listed below.

```
data work.sales2001(keep=EmployeeID EmployeeGroup EmployeeManager
                         OrderDate SaleAmount Commission SaleMonth);
   set univ.dailysales2001;
   Commission = SaleAmount * 0.03;
   SaleMonth = scan(OrderDate,2,'-');
run;


title '2001 Sales and Salaries for Sales Teams';
proc print data=sales2001 noobs label;
   var OrderDate EmployeeManager EmployeeGroup Commission SaleAmount;
   format Commission SaleAmount dollar9.2;
   label OrderDate='Date of Order'
         EmployeeManager='Manager ID'
         SaleAmount='Sales Revenue';
run;
```

b. Use IF-THEN logic to modify the values of **SaleMonth**. Add the appropriate statements that change the values from the three-letter abbreviation to the full word. Set an appropriate length for **SaleMonth**.

c. Alter the PROC PRINT step to create the detail report displayed below.

Partial SAS Output

```
                        2001 Sales for Sales Teams

                  Month
                  of                               Sales
                  Sale       Commission           Revenue

                  January        $1.04             $34.50
                  January        $1.59             $53.00
                  January        $0.56             $18.80
                  January        $4.24            $141.20
                  January        $0.48             $16.00
                  January       $29.54            $984.50
                  January        $6.60            $220.00
```

d. Create the summary report displayed below and then save your work as **ch3ex3.sas**.

SAS Output

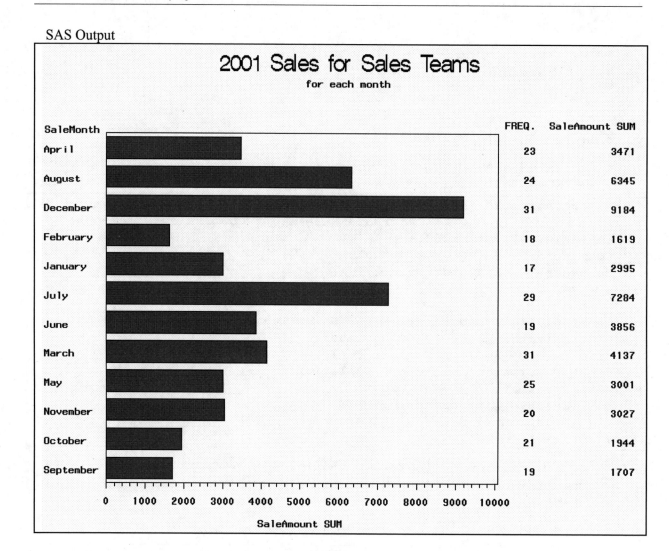

3.4 Using a Simple DO Loop to Process Data

Objectives

- Understand DO loop processing.
- Eliminate redundant code.

53

Introduction

DO loops can be used to do the following:

- perform repetitive calculations
- generate data
- eliminate redundant code
- execute SAS code conditionally
- read data

54

Business Need

Orion Star wants to encourage employees to save for retirement.

If 6% of an employee's salary is invested in a 401(k) plan each year (not to exceed $11,000), how much money could be saved after 30, 40, and 50 years?

(Assume that the average return of the plan is 11%.)

55

Repetitive Processing

Partial DATA Step

```
data retire(keep = EmployeeID Salary Investment
                   Value_after_30_years
                   Value_after_40_years
                   Value_after_50_years);
   set univ.usemps;
   Retirement = 0;
   Investment = 0.06 * Salary;
   if Investment gt 11000 then Investment = 11000;
   *Year 1;
   Retirement = Retirement + Investment;
   Retirement = Retirement * 1.11;
   *Year 2;
   Retirement = Retirement + Investment;
   Retirement = Retirement * 1.11;
   *Year 3;
        .
        .
        .
   *Year 30;
   Retirement = Retirement + Investment;
   Retirement = Retirement * 1.11;
   Value_after_30_years = Retirement;
```

56   c03s4d1.sas

DO Loop Syntax

General form of a simple iterative DO loop:

DO *index-variable=start* TO *stop* <BY *increment*>;
   SAS statements
END;

57

The *start*, *stop*, and *increment* values

- are established upon entry into the DO loop
- cannot be changed during the processing of the DO loop
- can be numbers, variables, or SAS expressions

The value of the *index-variable* can be changed within the loop.

The default increment is 1.

DO Loop Processing

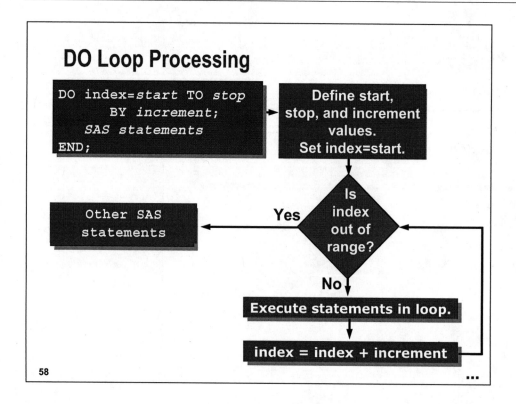

```
DO index=start TO stop
    BY increment;
  SAS statements
END;
```

Define start, stop, and increment values. Set index=start.

Is index out of range?

Yes

Other SAS statements

No

Execute statements in loop.

index = index + increment

58   ...

DO Loop Syntax

You can define the values used to increment the loop with *start* **TO** *stop* **<BY** *increment***>**.

```
do i=2 to 10 by 2;
```

            2   4   6   8   10

```
do i=10 to 2 by -2;
```

            10   8   6   4   2

```
do k=3.6 to 3.8 by .05;
```

        3.6   3.65   3.70   3.75   3.80   3.85

59   ...

DO Loop Syntax

Expressions:

```
do z=k to n/10;
```

Dates:

```
do date='01JAN2003'd to '31JAN2003'd;
```

60

The date constant '*ddMMMyyyy*'d creates a SAS date value from the date enclosed in quotes.

DO Loop Syntax

General form of a DO loop with a value list:

DO *index-variable=value1, value2, value3...;*
    SAS statements
END;

The values in the list can be numeric or character.

61

DO Loop Syntax

Discrete numeric values separated by commas:

```
do n=1,5,15,30,60;
```

Character values enclosed in quotes and separated by commas:

```
do month='JAN','FEB','MAR';
```

62

DO Loop Code

```
data retire(keep = EmployeeID Salary Investment
                   Value_after_30_years
                   Value_after_40_years
                   Value_after_50_years);
   set univ.usemps;
   Retirement = 0;
   Investment = 0.06 * Salary;
   if Investment gt 11000 then Investment = 11000;
   do year = 1 to 50;
      /* Add the Investment amount each year */
      Retirement = Retirement + Investment;
      Retirement= Retirement * 1.11;
       /* Retirement value after 30, 40 and 50 years */
      if Year = 30 then
         Value_after_30_years = Retirement;
       else if Year = 40 then
         Value_after_40_years = Retirement;
       else if Year = 50 then
         Value_after_50_years = Retirement;
   end;
run;
```

63   c03s4d1.sas

The DATA step is a looping process. DO loops iterate within the normal processing of the DATA step loop, and perform repetitive execution of the same statement or statements.

Performing Repetitive Calculations

c03s4d1.sas

Orion Star wants to encourage employees to save for retirement.

Calculate the amount that each employee could save if they invest 6% of their salary in a 401(k) plan each year (not to exceed $11,000) for 30, 40, and 50 years. (Assume that the average return of the plan is 11%.)

1. Create a new data set named **retire** based on the **univ.usemps** data set.

   - Create a new variable named **Retirement** that should be initialized to 0.

   - Create a new variable named **Investment** that is 6% of the employee's salary. Add a condition to set the investment to $11,000 if 6% of the salary exceeds $11,000.

   - Use DO loop statements to do the following:

   a. Add the value of the variable **Investment** to the value of **Retirement**.

   b. Apply the 11% increase to the value of **Retirement**.

   c. Create three variables, **Value_after_30_years**, **Value_after_40_years**, and **Value_after_50_years** that are based on the values of **Retirement**.

   - Keep only the variables **EmployeeID**, **Salary**, **Investment**, **Value_after_30_years**, **Value_after_40_years**, and **Value_after_50_years** in the **retire** data set.

```
data retire(keep=EmployeeID Salary Investment
                 Value_after_30_years Value_after_40_years
                 Value_after_50_years);
   set univ.usemps;

   Retirement=0;
   Investment=0.06 * Salary;
   if Investment gt 11000 then Investment = 11000;
   do year=1 to 50;
      /* Add the Investment amount each year */
      Retirement=Retirement + Investment;
      Retirement=Retirement * 1.11;
    /* Want to see the Retirement value after 30, 40 and 50 years */
     if Year=30 then
        Value_after_30_years=Retirement;
     else if Year=40 then
        Value_after_40_years=Retirement;
     else if Year=50 then
        Value_after_50_years=Retirement;
   end;
run;
```

2. Use the PRINT procedure to create a report of the retirement values for each employee after 30, 40, and 50 years.

```
title 'Retirement Projections for Investments after 30, 40 and 50
Years';

proc print data=retire noobs label;
  var EmployeeID Investment Value_after_30_years
        Value_after_40_years Value_after_50_years;
  format value_after_30_years value_after_40_years
           value_after_50_years dollar15.2;
  label EmployeeID='Employee ID'
          Investment='Amount Invested Each Year'
          Value_after_30_years = 'Value After 30 Years'
          Value_after_40_years = 'Value After 40 Years'
          Value_after_50_years = 'Value After 50 Years';
run;
```

Partial SAS Output

		Retirement Projections for Investments after 30, 40 and 50 Years		
Employee ID	Amount Invested Each Year	Value After 30 Years	Value After 40 Years	Value After 50 Years
00121084	1362.6	$301,016.29	$880,003.78	$2,523,993.00
00121064	1506.6	$332,827.79	$973,002.86	$2,790,729.39
00121057	1507.5	$333,026.61	$973,584.10	$2,792,396.49
00121044	1539.6	$340,117.92	$994,315.15	$2,851,856.47
00121092	1540.8	$340,383.02	$995,090.14	$2,854,079.28
00121079	1546.2	$341,575.95	$998,577.60	$2,864,081.89
00121106	1552.8	$343,033.98	$1,002,840.06	$2,876,307.31
00121051	1561.5	$344,955.92	$1,008,458.76	$2,892,422.63
00121109	1562.1	$345,088.47	$1,008,846.25	$2,893,534.03
00121041	1567.2	$346,215.13	$1,012,139.97	$2,902,980.95
00121027	1569.9	$346,811.59	$1,013,883.70	$2,907,982.25
00121069	1571.7	$347,209.24	$1,015,046.19	$2,911,316.46
00121058	1576.2	$348,203.35	$1,017,952.41	$2,919,651.97
00121096	1580.1	$349,064.91	$1,020,471.14	$2,926,876.08

Exercises

The suppliers to Orion Star Sports & Outdoors have announced a 2% increase on the invoice price of goods over the next five years. It has been proposed that Orion Star not raise its prices for five years to remain competitive. Determine the potential net revenue losses at the end of five years based on the sales from 2001. Assume that the commission rate will remain 3% for the next five years and that the invoice price will increase by 2% each year for five years.

4. **Creating a Variable Using DO Loop Processing**

   a. Recall the DATA step that created **work.sales2001** in the previous exercise. If necessary, include **ch3ex3.sas** or **bkup33.sas**.

```
data work.sales2001(keep= EmployeeID EmployeeGroup EmployeeManager
                          OrderDate SaleAmount Commission SaleMonth);
   set univ.dailysales2001;
   length SaleMonth $ 10;
   Commission=SaleAmount * 0.03;
   SaleMonth=scan (OrderDate,2,'-');
   if SaleMonth='JAN' then SaleMonth='January';
   else if SaleMonth='FEB' then SaleMonth='February';
   else if SaleMonth='MAR' then SaleMonth='March';
   else if SaleMonth='APR' then SaleMonth='April';
   else if SaleMonth='MAY' then SaleMonth='May';
   else if SaleMonth='JUN' then SaleMonth='June';
   else if SaleMonth='JUL' then SaleMonth='July';
   else if SaleMonth='AUG' then SaleMonth='August';
   else if SaleMonth='SEP' then SaleMonth='September';
   else if SaleMonth='OCT' then SaleMonth='October';
   else if SaleMonth='NOV' then SaleMonth='November';
   else if SaleMonth='DEC' then SaleMonth='December';
run;
```

   b. Modify this code by creating three new variables: **Invoice2001**, **InvoicePrice**, and **PotRevLoss**.

      - **Invoice2001** is the current invoice price (in 2001), which is 60% of the **SaleAmount**.

      - **InvoicePrice** is the invoice price at the end of five years with a 2% increase each year.

      - **PotRevLoss** is difference between the current invoice price and the invoice price in five years.

   c. Use DO loop processing to calculate the values of **Invoice2001**, **InvoicePrice**, and **PotRevLoss** at the end of five years.

d. Use the PRINT procedure to generate the list report displayed below.

e. Save the DATA step and PROC PRINT step as **ch3ex4.sas**.

SAS Output

```
                       Potential Losses in 5 years based on 2001 Sales
                                   if prices remain frozen


                                                       Potential
                                           Current      Future     Potential
           Month of                        Invoice      Invoice    2006 Revenue
             Sale      SaleAmount           Price        Price        Loss

           January       $34.50            $20.70       $22.85       $-2.15
           January       $53.00            $31.80       $35.11       $-3.31
           January       $18.80            $11.28       $12.45       $-1.17
           January      $141.20            $84.72       $93.54       $-8.82
           January       $16.00             $9.60       $10.60       $-1.00
           January      $984.50           $590.70      $652.18      $-61.48
           January      $220.00           $132.00      $145.74      $-13.74
           January      $112.00            $67.20       $74.19       $-6.99
           January      $259.60           $155.76      $171.97      $-16.21
           January       $78.80            $47.28       $52.20       $-4.92
           January      $144.50            $86.70       $95.72       $-9.02
           January      $141.20            $84.72       $93.54       $-8.82
           January      $142.30            $85.38       $94.27       $-8.89
           January       $18.20            $10.92       $12.06       $-1.14
           January      $470.80           $282.48      $311.88      $-29.40
           January       $63.00            $37.80       $41.73       $-3.93
           January       $96.60            $57.96       $63.99       $-6.03
           February     $124.00            $74.40       $82.14       $-7.74
           February     $134.00            $80.40       $88.77       $-8.37
           February     $141.90            $85.14       $94.00       $-8.86
           February      $29.40            $17.64       $19.48       $-1.84
```

3.5 SAS Array Processing

Objectives

- Understand the concepts of SAS arrays.
- Use SAS arrays to perform repetitive calculations.

Performing Repetitive Calculations

Employees contribute an amount to charity every quarter. The SAS data set `univ.donate` contains contribution data for each employee. The employer supplements each contribution by 25 percent.

Calculate each employee's quarterly contribution including the company supplement.

Partial Listing of `univ.donate`

ID	Qtr1	Qtr2	Qtr3	Qtr4
E00224	12	33	22	.
E00367	35	48	40	30

Performing Repetitive Calculations

```
data charity;
   set univ.donate;
   Qtr1=Qtr1*1.25;
   Qtr2=Qtr2*1.25;
   Qtr3=Qtr3*1.25;
   Qtr4=Qtr4*1.25;
run;

proc print data=charity noobs;
run;
```

69   c03s5d1.sas

Performing Repetitive Calculations

Partial PROC PRINT Output

ID	Qtr1	Qtr2	Qtr3	Qtr4
E00224	15.00	41.25	27.50	.
E00367	43.75	60.00	50.00	37.50
E00441	.	78.75	111.25	112.50
E00587	20.00	23.75	37.50	36.25
E00598	5.00	10.00	7.50	1.25

What if you want to similarly modify 52 weeks of data stored in **Week1** through **Week52**?

70

Array Processing

You can use arrays to simplify programs that

- perform repetitive calculations
- create many variables with the same attributes
- read data
- rotate SAS data sets by making variables into observations or observations into variables
- compare variables
- perform a table lookup

71

What Is a SAS Array?

A *SAS array*

- is a temporary grouping of SAS variables that are arranged in a particular order
- is identified by an *array name*
- exists only for the duration of the current DATA step
- is **not** a variable

72

SAS arrays are different from arrays in many other programming languages. In SAS, an array is **not** a data structure, but a convenient way of temporarily identifying a group of variables.

What Is a SAS Array?

Each value in an array is

- called an *element*
- identified by a *subscript* that represents the position of the element in the array.

When you use an *array reference*, the corresponding value is substituted for the reference.

73

What Is a SAS Array?

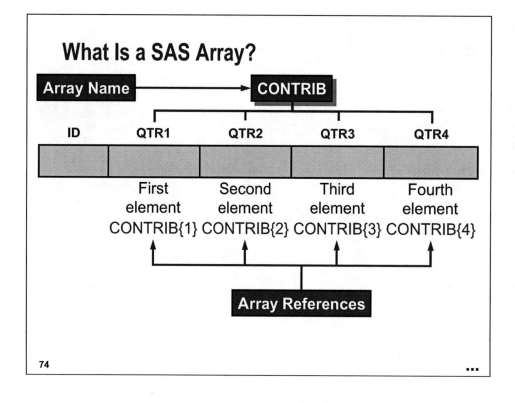

74

The ARRAY Statement

The ARRAY statement defines the elements in an array. These elements are processed as a group. You refer to elements of the array by the array name and subscript.

> **ARRAY** *array-name {subscript}* <$> *<length>*
> *<array-elements> <(initial-value-list)>*;

75

array-name	specifies the name of the array.
{subscript}	describes the number and arrangement of elements in the array by using an asterisk, a number, or a range of numbers. *subscript* is enclosed in braces ({}). Brackets ([]) and parentheses (()) are also allowed. *subscript* often has the form *{dimension-size(s)}*. *{dimension-size(s)}* is used to indicate a numeric representation of either the number of elements in a one-dimensional array or the number of elements in each dimension of a multidimensional array.
$	indicates that the elements in the array are character elements. The dollar sign is not necessary if the elements in the array were previously defined as character elements.
length	specifies the length of elements in the array that were not previously assigned a length.
array-elements	names the elements that make up the array. Array elements can be listed in any order.
(initial-value-list)	gives initial values for the corresponding elements in the array. The values for elements can be numbers or character strings. You must enclose all character strings in quotation marks.

✎ Array names cannot be used in LABEL, FORMAT, DROP, KEEP, or LENGTH statements.

If you use a function name as the name of the array, SAS treats parenthetical references that involve the name as array references, not function references, for the duration of the DATA step.

The ARRAY Statement

The ARRAY statement

- must contain all numeric or all character elements
- must be used to define an array before the array name can be referenced
- creates variables if they do not already exist in the PDV
- is a compile-time statement

76

You can use special SAS name lists to reference variables that were previously defined in the same DATA step. The _CHARACTER_ variable lists character values only. The _NUMERIC_ variable lists numeric values only.

Avoid using the _ALL_ special SAS name list to reference variables because the elements in an array must be either all character or all numeric values.

Defining an Array

Write an ARRAY statement that defines the four quarterly contribution variables as elements of an array.

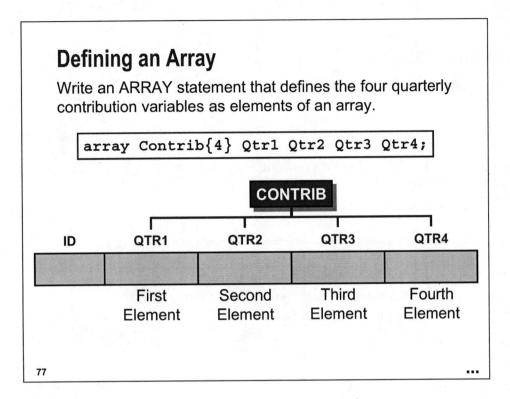

```
array Contrib{4} Qtr1 Qtr2 Qtr3 Qtr4;
```

77

The four variables **Qtr1**, **Qtr2**, **Qtr3**, and **Qtr4** can now be referenced by the array name **Contrib**.

Defining an Array

Variables that are elements of an array do not need to have similar, related, or numbered names.

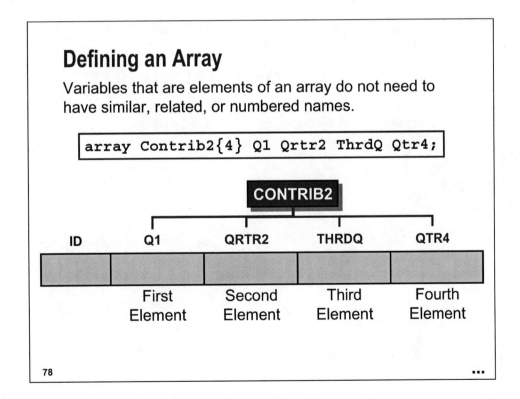

```
array Contrib2{4} Q1 Qrtr2 ThrdQ Qtr4;
```

78

Processing an Array

Array processing often occurs within DO loops.
An iterative DO loop that processes an array has
the following form:

```
DO index-variable=1 TO number-of-elements-in-array;
    additional SAS statements
        using array-name{index-variable}...
END;
```

To execute the loop as many times as there are elements
in the array, specify that the values of *index-variable*
range from 1 to *number-of-elements-in-array*.

79

You must tell SAS which variable in the array to use in each iteration of the loop. You can write programming statements so that the index variable of the DO loop is the subscript of the array reference (for example, *array-name{index-variable}*). When the value of the index variable changes, the subscript of the array reference (and therefore the variable that is referenced) also changes.

To process particular elements of an array, specify those elements as the range of the iterative DO statement.

By default, SAS includes *index-variable* in the output data set. Use a DROP statement or the DROP= data set option to prevent the index variable from being written to your output data set.

Processing an Array

```
array Contrib{4} Qtr1 Qtr2 Qtr3 Qtr4;
do Qtr = 1 to 4;
    Contrib{Qtr} = Contrib{Qtr}*1.25;
end;
```

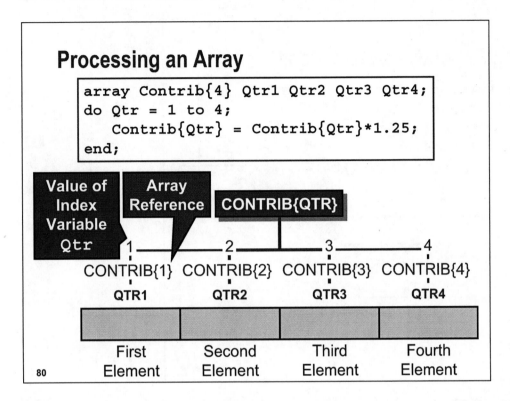

The name of the index variable, `Qtr`, was chosen for clarity. Any valid SAS variable name could be used.

Performing Repetitive Calculations

```
data charity(drop = Qtr);
   set univ.donate;
   array Contrib{4} Qtr1 Qtr2 Qtr3 Qtr4;
   do Qtr = 1 to 4;
      Contrib{Qtr} = Contrib{Qtr}*1.25;
   end;
run;
```

c03s5d1.sas

Performing Repetitive Calculations

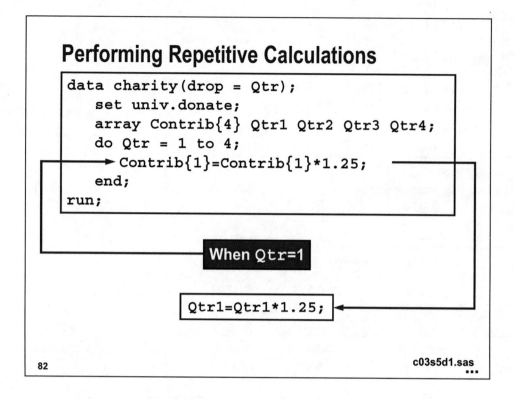

```
data charity(drop = Qtr);
   set univ.donate;
   array Contrib{4} Qtr1 Qtr2 Qtr3 Qtr4;
   do Qtr = 1 to 4;
        Contrib{1}=Contrib{1}*1.25;
   end;
run;
```

When Qtr=1

```
Qtr1=Qtr1*1.25;
```

82   c03s5d1.sas

Performing Repetitive Calculations

```
proc print data = charity noobs;
run;
```

Partial PROC PRINT Output

ID	Qtr1	Qtr2	Qtr3	Qtr4
E00224	15.00	41.25	27.50	.
E00367	43.75	60.00	50.00	37.50
E00441	.	78.75	111.25	112.50
E00587	20.00	23.75	37.50	36.25
E00598	5.00	10.00	7.50	1.25

86   c03s5d1.sas

Performing Repetitive Calculations Using Arrays

c03s5d1.sas

Calculate the amount of each employee's quarterly contributions to charity after adding a 25 percent employer-matching supplement.

```
data charity(drop=Qtr);
   set univ.donate;
   array Contrib{4} Qtr1 Qtr2 Qtr3 Qtr4;
   do Qtr=1 to 4;
      Contrib{Qtr}=Contrib{Qtr}*1.25;
   end;
run;

proc print data=charity noobs;
   title 'Contributions after 25 percent supplement';
run;
```

Partial SAS Output

```
         Contributions after 25 percent supplement

        ID       Qtr1      Qtr2      Qtr3      Qtr4

        E00224   15.00     41.25     27.50       .
        E00367   43.75     60.00     50.00     37.50
        E00441       .     78.75    111.25    112.50
        E00587   20.00     23.75     37.50     36.25
        E00598    5.00     10.00      7.50      1.25
        E00621   12.50     15.00     18.75     31.25
        E00630   83.75    107.50     65.00    105.00
        E00705   11.25      8.75     61.25      2.50
        E00727   10.00     33.75     31.25     17.50
        E00860   12.50     18.75      7.50     25.00
        E00901   23.75     26.25      3.75     30.00
```

Exercises

5. Using Arrays for Repetitive Computations (Optional)

Information on the different product categories that each supplier furnishes to Orion Star Sports & Outdoors is contained in the data set **univ.suppliercategories**. Indicators for each of 12 product categories are set to Yes if the supplier supplies at least one item in that category.

Partial Listing of **univ.suppliercategories**

SupplierName	Assorted Sports Articles	Children Sports	Clothes	Golf	Indoor Sports
3Top Sports	NO	yEs	yeS	no	No
A Team Sports	YES	yeS	Yes	no	no
AllSeasons Outdoor Clothing	yes	yEs	yeS	no	no
Bon Garrments	yes	no	no	No	no
British Sports Ltd	no	no	no	no	no
Carolina Sports	no	nO	no	Yes	no
CrystalClear Optics Inc	yEs	no	no	no	no
Dolphin Sportswear Inc	no	no	no	no	no
Eclipse Inc	no	yes	yes	no	no
Force Sports	no	no	no	no	no

Outdoors	Racket Sports	Running_ Jogging	Shoes	Swim Sports	Team Sports	Winter Sports
nO	no	yeS	YEs	no	no	no
No	no	yes	no	no	No	no
YEs	no	no	no	No	no	no
no	no	no	no	no	NO	no
no	yeS	no	no	no	no	no
no	nO	no	no	no	no	no
no	no	no	no	no	no	NO
no	no	NO	no	yes	no	no
no	no	no	yEs	no	no	no
no	no	yes	no	no	no	no

For example, A Team Sports provides AssortedSportsArticles, ChildrenSports, Clothes and Running_Jogging products, while Carolina Sports provides only Golf products.

a. Create a new temporary data set named **countWithLoop** by reading the **univ.suppliercategories** data set.

b. Use an iterative DO loop to create a variable **NumOfProdCategories** that counts the number of product categories that each company supplies to Orion Star Sports & Outdoors.

c. Use the PRINT procedure to examine the values of **NumOfProdCategories**.

SAS Output

Obs	SupplierName	NumOfProd Categories
1	3Top Sports	4
2	A Team Sports	4
3	AllSeasons Outdoor Clothing	4
4	Bon Garrments	1
5	British Sports Ltd	1
6	Carolina Sports	1
7	CrystalClear Optics Inc	1
8	Dolphin Sportswear Inc	1
9	Eclipse Inc	3
10	Force Sports	1
11	Fuller Trading Co.	1
12	GrandSlam Sporting Goods Ltd	2
13	Green Lime Sports Inc	1
14	Greenline Sports Ltd	2
15	Harry Penny Ltd	1
16	HighPoint Trading	0
17	KN Outdoor Trading Inc	1
18	Le Blanc S.A.	1
19	Luna sastreria S.A.	4
20	Magnifico Sports	1
21	Massif S.A.	1
22	Mayday Inc	3
23	Miller Trading Inc	1
24	Nautlius SportsWear Inc	1
25	Norsok A/S	1
26	Outback Outfitters Ltd	1
27	Petterson AB	2
28	Pro Sportswear Inc	1
29	Roll-Over Inc	1
30	SD Sporting Goods Inc	2
31	Scandinavian Clothing A/S	1
32	Sockeye Sportswear Inc	1
33	Sportico	1
34	Teamsports Inc	1
35	Top Sports	1
36	Top Sports Inc	1
37	Toto Outdoor Gear	1
38	Triffy B.V.	1
39	Triple Sportswear Inc	2
40	Truls Sporting Goods	1
41	Twain Inc	4
42	Typhoon Clothing	1
43	Ultra Sporting Goods Inc	1
44	Van Dammeren International	2
45	Ypsilon S.A.	1

3.6 Subsetting Data Rows

Objectives

- Explain the subsetting IF statement.
- Explain the WHERE statement.

90

Subsetting Data in the DATA Step

To produce numerous reports on a subset of data in a SAS data set,

- create a new data set with the desired data
- process the new data set with SAS procedures

91

The Subsetting IF Statement

You can use a subsetting IF statement to determine which rows are written to the SAS data set.

General form of the subsetting IF statement:

IF *expression*;

The *expression* can be any SAS expression.

92

Process Flow of a Subsetting IF

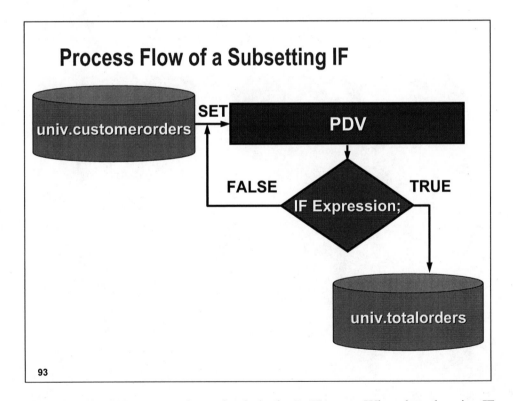

93

The subsetting IF statement is used only in the DATA step. When the subsetting IF statement is used, the condition is checked after the observation is read into the PDV. If the condition is true, SAS continues processing the observation. If the condition is false, the observation is discarded and processing continues with the next observation.

Selecting Rows Conditionally

The subsetting IF statement is valid

- only in a DATA step
- when the variable that is used to select observations is
  - created from a raw data file when an INPUT statement is used
  - created by an assignment statement
  - obtained from an existing SAS data set

94

Selecting Observations Using a Subsetting IF Statement

c03s6d1.sas

Create a new data set named **univ.totalorders** from the **univ.customerorders** data set that contains only valid data values for the variable **Quantity**.

- Use a subsetting IF statement to include selected observations in a SAS data set and eliminate unwanted observations.
- Use the PRINT procedure to generate an enhanced list report.

1. Use a subsetting IF statement in a DATA step to eliminate bad or missing data from being passed to the data set being created.

2. Create a new variable that calculates the final billing amount for those observations that meet the subsetting IF criteria.

3. Submit the program for execution and browse the log.

```
data univ.totalorders (drop=OrderDate OrderID ProductID);
   set univ.customerorders;
   length Level $9;
   TotalSale=UnitPrice*Quantity;
   if Quantity in (1,2) then do;
      Level='Level I';
      Discountaward=0;
   end;
   else if Quantity=3 then do;
      Level='Level II';
      Discountaward=TotalSale*.05;
   end;
   else if Quantity ge 4 then do;
      Level='Level III';
      Discountaward=TotalSale*.10;
   end;
   else Level='Miscoded';
   if Level ne 'Miscoded';
   Billedamount=TotalSale-Discountaward;
run;
```

4. The log indicates that 201 observations were read from **univ.customerorders**, and 198 were written to **univ.totalorders**, indicating that there were 3 records that had bad data, missing data, or a value of 0 for the variable **Quantity**.

Partial Log

```
NOTE: Missing values were generated as a result of performing an operation on missing values.
      Each place is given by: (Number of times) at (Line):(Column).
      2 at 242:23
NOTE: There were 201 observations read from the data set UNIV.CUSTOMERORDERS.
NOTE: The data set UNIV.TOTALORDERS has 198 observations and 7 variables.
```

5. Use PROC PRINT to create the list report displayed below.

```
title ' Final Billed Amounts After Discounts';
proc print data=univ.totalorders noobs label;
   var Level BilledAmount;
   format BilledAmount dollar9.;
   label Billedamount='Final Sale Amount';
run;
```

Partial SAS Output

```
                   Final Billed Amounts After Discounts

                                       Final
                                       Sale
                      Level           Amount

                      Level III         $468
                      Level I           $122
                      Level I           $468
                      Level I            $87
                      Level I           $181
                      Level I           $135
                      Level I            $23
                      Level I            $38
                      Level I            $50
                      Level I           $264
```

6. Use PROC GCHART to create the list report displayed below.

```
proc gchart data=univ.totalorders;
   vbar level / sumvar=BilledAmount;
run;
quit;
```

SAS Output

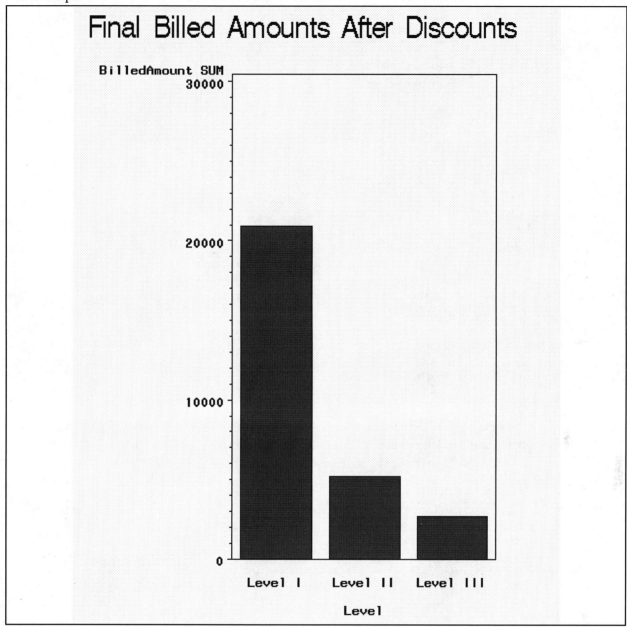

```
data univ.Totalorders (drop= OrderDate OrderID ProductID)
    invaliddata;
    set univ.customerorders;
    length Level $9;
    TotalSale=UnitPrice*Quantity;
    if Quantity in (1,2)then do;
        Level='Level I';
        Discountaward=0;
    end;
    else if Quantity=3 then do;
        Level= 'Level II';
        Discountaward=TotalSale*.05;
    end;
    else if Quantity ge 4 then do;
        Level='Level III';
        Discountaward=TotalSale*.10;
    end;
    else do;
        Level='Miscoded';
        output invaliddata;
    end;
    if Level ne 'Miscoded';
    Billedamount=TotalSale-Discountaward;
    output univ.totalorders;
run;
```

In the DATA step above, the invalid records that were not included in the new data set could be written out to another data set so that they could be investigated later. An OUTPUT statement in combination with the DATA statement produces these results.

Partial Log

```
NOTE: Missing values were generated as a result of performing an operation on missing values.
      Each place is given by: (Number of times) at (Line):(Column).
      2 at 320:23
NOTE: There were 201 observations read from the data set UNIV.CUSTOMERORDERS.
NOTE: The data set UNIV.TOTALORDERS has 198 observations and 10 variables.
NOTE: The data set WORK.INVALIDDATA has 3 observations and 10 variables.
NOTE: DATA statement used (Total process time):
      real time          0.03 seconds
      cpu time           0.03 seconds
```

If there is at least **one** OUTPUT statement in the DATA step, SAS will **not** automatically output at the bottom of the DATA step.

If an OUPUT statement is used without specifying a data set name, SAS will output to **all** data sets listed in the DATA statement.

Subsetting Data in the PROC Step

You can use a WHERE statement to determine which rows are read by SAS for further processing.

General form of the WHERE statement:

> **WHERE** *expression*;

The expression can be any valid SAS expression.

96

The WHERE Statement

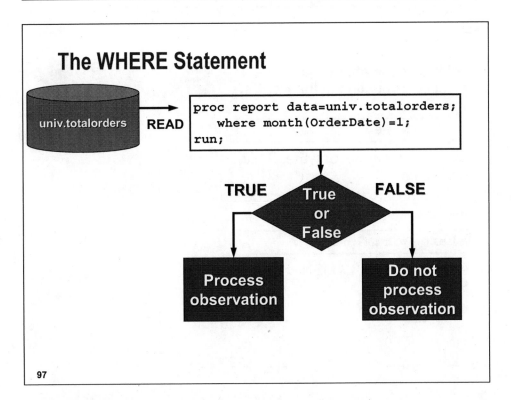

97

7.   A WHERE expression can be used in both DATA and PROC steps. A WHERE expression tests the condition before the observation is read into the PDV. If the condition is true, the observation is read into the PDV and processed. If the condition is false, the observation is not read into the PDV, and processing continues with the next observation.

Special Operators

The following are special operators:

LIKE selects observations by comparing character values to specified patterns. A percent sign (%) replaces any number of characters and an underscore (_) replaces one character.

```
where Code like 'E_U%';
```

(E, a single character, U, followed by any characters.)

98

continued...

Special Operators

=*   selects observations that contain a spelling variation of the word(s) specified.

```
where Name=*'SMITH';
```

selects the names Smythe, Smitt, and so on.

CONTAINS or ? selects observations that include the specified substring.

```
where Word ? 'LAM';
```

selects BLAME, LAMENT, and BEDLAM.

99

continued...

Special Operators

IS NULL or IS MISSING

> selects observations in which the value of the variable is missing.

```
where quantity is missing;
```

BETWEEN-AND selects observations in which the value of the variable falls within a range of values.

```
where date between '01mar2003'd
       and '01apr2003'd;
```

100

Selecting Observations for a Report Using a WHERE Statement

c03s6d2.sas

Create a report that shows only the first quarter customer data. Display the results in a list report.

- Use the PRINT procedure to generate an enhanced list report.
- Use a WHERE statement to include selected observations in the report.

```
title 'First Quarter Orders';
proc print data=univ.customerorders noobs label;
   where month(OrderDate) in (1,2,3);
   format Quantity 3.;
   label CustomerId='Customer ID';
run;
```

Partial SAS Output

Customer ID	ProductID	Quantity
032096	220100200011	1
032096	240500100017	1
035901	220200100113	1
035901	240100400106	1
036324	230100200006	1
036324	230100600005	1
040441	220200100113	1
044817	220101400056	1
047675	220100100380	1
047675	220100100523	1
047675	210200500018	1
047675	220200100098	3
047675	220200100222	1
049576	220100800012	.
049576	220101400313	1
049576	220101200031	1
049576	220100100634	1
049576	220200200042	1
050759	230100100058	2
051347	220200100122	1
051347	220101000004	1
053220	240500100039	1
053220	240700200018	1
053220	220100500018	1
053220	240800200047	2

First Quarter Orders

Exercises

6. Using a WHERE Statement to Subset Observations for a Report

Recall the PROC PRINT step that displays the potential losses if prices remain frozen while invoice prices increase over five years. If necessary, include **ch3ex4.sas** or **bkup34.sas**.

```
title 'Potential 3rd Quarter Losses in 2006';

proc print data=sales2001 noobs label;
   var SaleMonth  SaleAmount Invoice2001
           InvoicePrice PotRevLoss;
   format SaleAmount PotRevLoss dollar12.2
           Invoice2001 InvoicePrice dollar10.2;
     label SaleMonth='Month of Sale'
           SaleAmount='Sales Revenue'
           Invoice2001='CurrentInvoicePrice'
           InvoicePrice='Potential Future Invoice Price'
           PotRevLoss='Potential 2006 Revenue Loss'
run;
```

Orion Star Sports & Outdoors traditionally has its highest sales in the third quarter, in July, August, and September. Modify the program to report only the sales from July, August, and September.

Partial SAS Output

			Potential	
		Current	Future	Potential
Month of	Sales	Invoice	Invoice	2006 Revenue
Sale	Revenue	Price	Price	Loss
July	$1,133.20	$679.92	$750.69	$-70.77
July	$26.20	$15.72	$17.36	$-1.64
July	$86.80	$52.08	$57.50	$-5.42
July	$144.90	$86.94	$95.99	$-9.05
July	$48.80	$29.28	$32.33	$-3.05
July	$251.80	$151.08	$166.80	$-15.72
July	$205.50	$123.30	$136.13	$-12.83
July	$181.20	$108.72	$120.04	$-11.32
July	$191.00	$114.60	$126.53	$-11.93
July	$190.10	$114.06	$125.93	$-11.87

Potential 3rd Quarter Losses in 2006

3.7 Solutions to Exercises

1. Using the DATA Step to Create a SAS Data Set

```
data work.sales2001(keep=EmployeeID EmployeeGroup EmployeeManager
                         OrderDate SaleAmount);
   set univ.dailysales2001;
run;


proc print data=work.sales2001;
run;
```

2. Creating New Variables

```
data work.sales2001(keep=EmployeeID EmployeeGroup EmployeeManager
                         OrderDate SaleAmount Commission SaleMonth);
   set univ.dailysales2001;
   Commission = SaleAmount * 0.03;
   SaleMonth = scan(OrderDate,2,'-');
run;


proc contents data=work.sales2001;
run;


title '2001 Sales and Salaries for Sales Teams';
proc print data=sales2001 noobs label;
   var OrderDate EmployeeManager EmployeeGroup Commission SaleAmount;
   format Commission SaleAmount dollar9.2;
   label OrderDate='Date of Order'
     EmployeeManager='Manager ID'
          SaleAmount='Sales Revenue';
run;


title2 'for each month';
proc gchart data=sales2001;
  vbar Salemonth / sumvar= SaleAmount;
  run;
quit;
```

3. Modifying Values Using IF-THEN Logic

```
data work.sales2001(keep=EmployeeID EmployeeGroup EmployeeManager
                          OrderDate SaleAmount Commission SaleMonth);
   set univ.dailysales2001;
   length SaleMonth $ 10;
   Commission = SaleAmount * 0.03;
   SaleMonth = scan (OrderDate,2,'-');
   if SaleMonth = 'JAN' then SaleMonth = 'January';
   else if SaleMonth = 'FEB' then SaleMonth = 'February';
   else if SaleMonth = 'MAR' then SaleMonth = 'March';
   else if SaleMonth = 'APR' then SaleMonth = 'April';
   else if SaleMonth = 'MAY' then SaleMonth = 'May';
   else if SaleMonth = 'JUN' then SaleMonth = 'June';
   else if SaleMonth = 'JUL' then SaleMonth = 'July';
   else if SaleMonth = 'AUG' then SaleMonth = 'August';
   else if SaleMonth = 'SEP' then SaleMonth = 'September';
   else if SaleMonth = 'OCT' then SaleMonth = 'October';
   else if SaleMonth = 'NOV' then SaleMonth = 'November';
   else if SaleMonth = 'DEC' then SaleMonth = 'December';
run;

title '2001 Sales and Salaries for Sales Teams';
proc print data=sales2001 noobs label;
   var SaleMonth Commission SaleAmount;
   format Commission SaleAmount dollar9.2;
   label SaleMonth='Month of Sale'
         SaleAMount='Sales Revenue';
run;

title2 'for each month';
proc gchart data=sales2001;
   hbar SaleMonth / sumvar=SaleAmount;
run;
quit;
```

4. Creating a Variable Using DO Loop Processing

```
data work.sales2001(keep=EmployeeID EmployeeGroup EmployeeManager
                          OrderDate SaleAmount Commission SaleMonth
                          Invoice2001 InvoicePrice PotRevLoss);
    set univ.dailysales2001;
    length SaleMonth $ 10;
    Commission = SaleAmount * 0.03;
    SaleMonth = scan (OrderDate,2,'-');
    if SaleMonth = 'JAN' then SaleMonth = 'January';
    else if SaleMonth = 'FEB' then SaleMonth = 'February';
    else if SaleMonth = 'MAR' then SaleMonth = 'March';
    else if SaleMonth = 'APR' then SaleMonth = 'April';
    else if SaleMonth = 'MAY' then SaleMonth = 'May';
    else if SaleMonth = 'JUN' then SaleMonth = 'June';
    else if SaleMonth = 'JUL' then SaleMonth = 'July';
    else if SaleMonth = 'AUG' then SaleMonth = 'August';
    else if SaleMonth = 'SEP' then SaleMonth = 'September';
    else if SaleMonth = 'OCT' then SaleMonth = 'October';
    else if SaleMonth = 'NOV' then SaleMonth = 'November';
    else if SaleMonth = 'DEC' then SaleMonth = 'December';
    Invoice2001 = 0.6*SaleAmount;
    InvoicePrice = Invoice2001;
    do i = 1 to 5;
        InvoicePrice = (0.02*InvoicePrice) + InvoicePrice;
         PotRevLoss=  Invoice2001 - InvoicePrice;
    end;
run;

title 'Potential Losses in 5 years based on 2001 Sales';
title2 'if prices remain frozen';
proc print data=sales2001 noobs label;
    var SaleMonth SaleAmount Invoice2001
            InvoicePrice PotRevLoss;
    format SaleAmount PotRevLoss dollar12.2
            Invoice2001 InvoicePrice dollar10.2;
    label SaleMonth='Month of Sale'
            SaleAmount='Sales Revenue'
            Invoice2001='Current Invoice Price'
            InvoicePrice='Potential Future InvoicePrice'
           PotRevLoss='Potential 2006 Revenue Loss';
run;
```

5. Using Arrays for Repetitive Computations (Optional)

```
data countWithLoop;
   set univ.suppliercategories;
   NumOfProdCategories=0;
   array Categories {12} AssortedSportsArticles ChildrenSports Clothes
                         Golf IndoorSports Outdoors RacketSports
                         Running_Jogging Shoes SwimSports TeamSports
                         WinterSports;
   do i=1 to 12;
      if upcase(Categories{i})='YES' then
         NumOfProdCategories = NumOfProdCategories + 1;
   end;
run;

proc print data=countWithLoop;
   var SupplierName NumOfProdCategories;
run;
```

6. Using a WHERE Statement to Subset Observations for a Report

```
title 'Potential 3rd Quarter Losses in 2006';

proc print data=sales2001 noobs label;
   var SaleMonth  SaleAmount Invoice2001
           InvoicePrice PotRevLoss;
   format SaleAmount PotRevLoss dollar12.2
           Invoice2001 InvoicePrice dollar10.2;
     label SaleMonth='Month of Sale'
           SaleAmount='Sales Revenue'
           Invoice2001='CurrentInvoicePrice'
           InvoicePrice='Potential Future Invoice Price'
           PotRevLoss='Potential 2006 Revenue Loss';
   where SaleMonth = 'July' or SaleMonth = 'August' or
         SaleMonth = 'September';
run;
```

Chapter 4   Working with Existing SAS Data Sets

4.1   Concatenating and Interleaving SAS Data Sets 4-3

4.2   Match-Merging SAS Data Sets 4-15

4.3   Solutions to Exercises 4-26

4.1   Concatenating and Interleaving SAS Data Sets

Objectives

- Define concatenation.
- Define interleaving.
- Use the SET statement to concatenate multiple data sets.
- Use PROC SORT to prepare a data set for interleaving.
- Use the SET and BY statements to interleave SAS data sets.

3

Concatenation

A *concatenation*

- combines two or more data sets, one after the other, into a single data set
- uses the SET statement.

The new data set

- contains all observations from the original data sets in sequential order
- by default, contains all variables from the original data sets.

4

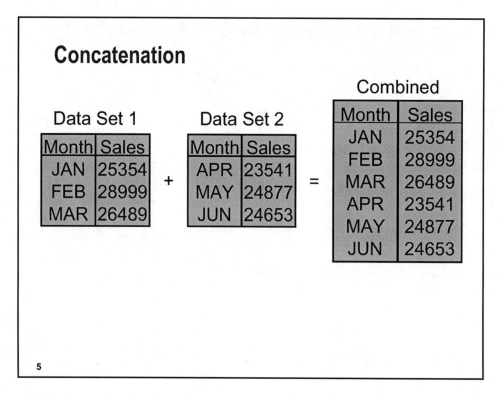

The newly created data set contains all the observations and all the variables from the original data sets. The observations are read sequentially from the data sets. Variables with the same name in each data set must be the same type.

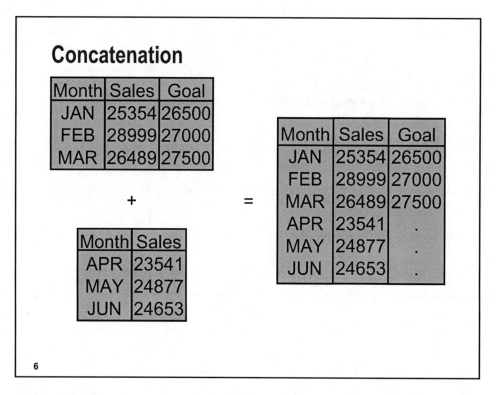

If the original data sets contain different variables, observations from one data set have missing values for variables defined only in other data sets.

Coding for Concatenation

Use the SET statement in a DATA step to concatenate SAS data sets.

General form of a DATA step concatenation:

```
DATA SAS-data-set ;
    SET SAS-data-set-1 SAS-data-set-2 ;
RUN;
```

7

Any number of data sets can be listed in the SET statement.

Observations from the original data sets are read into the new data set in the order the data sets are listed in the SET statement.

Concatenation Example

```
data univ.mastercustomers;
    set univ.uscustomers
        univ.usnewcustomers;
run;
```

c04s1d1.sas

8

Concatenating SAS Data Sets

c04s1d1.sas

Concatenate the **univ.uscustomers** and **univ.usnewcustomers** data sets to create the **univ.mastercustomers** data set.

1. Submit the DATA step to create the new data set.

```
data univ.mastercustomers;
   set univ.uscustomers univ.usnewcustomers;
run;
```

2. Examine the log to make sure that the program ran successfully without errors.

SAS Log

```
6    data univ.mastercustomers;
7       set univ.uscustomers univ.usnewcustomers;
8    run;

NOTE: There were 290 observations read from the data set UNIV.USCUSTOMERS.
NOTE: There were 20 observations read from the data set UNIV.USNEWCUSTOMERS.
NOTE: The data set UNIV.MASTERCUSTOMERS has 310 observations and 7 variables.
NOTE: DATA statement used (Total process time):
      real time          0.42 seconds
      cpu time           0.15 seconds
```

Neither data set is sorted.

Interleaving

Interleaving uses a SET statement and a BY statement to combine two or more SAS data sets.

The data set created through interleaving

- contains all observations from the original data sets
- is arranged by the values of the BY variable(s)
- by default, contains all variables from the original data sets.

10

Interleaving

Month	Sales
JAN	26510
FEB	24530
MAR	20122
MAR	14258

+

Month	Sales
JAN	21654
JAN	19873
FEB	22306
FEB	24003
MAR	19855
APR	23502

=

Month	Sales
JAN	26510
JAN	21654
JAN	19873
FEB	24530
FEB	22306
FEB	24003
MAR	20122
MAR	14258
MAR	19855
APR	23502

11

Sorting a SAS Data Set

Before you interleave SAS data sets, all data sets must be sorted on the variable(s) that determine(s) the order of observations in the final data set.

You can use PROC SORT to sort data.

General form of PROC SORT:

```
PROC SORT DATA=input-SAS-data-set
          OUT=output-SAS-data-set;
    BY <DESCENDING> by-variable(s);
RUN;
```

12

If the OUT= option is omitted, the DATA= data set is sorted and the sorted version replaces the original data set.

To sort variables in descending order, use the keyword DESCENDING in the BY statement before the name of each variable whose value you want sorted in descending order.

Sorting a SAS Data Set

The SORT procedure

- rearranges the observations in a SAS data set
- can create a new SAS data set that contains the rearranged observations
- can sort on multiple variables
- can sort in ascending (default) or descending order
- does not generate printed output
- treats missing values as the smallest possible value.

13

PROC SORT Example

```
proc sort data=univ.uscustomers
           out=uscustomers;
   by CustomerID;
run;

proc sort data=univ.usnewcustomers
           out=usnewcustomers;
   by CustomerID;
run;
```

c04s1d2.sas

14

Coding to Interleave SAS Data Sets

After the original data sets are properly sorted, the DATA step with a SET statement and a BY statement is used to interleave the sorted data sets.

General form of the DATA step:

```
DATA SAS-data-set;
    SET SAS-data-set-1 SAS-data-set-2;
    BY variable(s);
RUN;
```

15

Any number of SAS data sets can be listed in the SET statement.

Interleaving Example

```
data univ.mastercustomers;
   set uscustomers usnewcustomers;
   by CustomerID;
run;
```

16   c04s1d2.sas

Interleaving SAS Data Sets

c04s1d2.sas

Interleave **univ.uscustomers** and **univ.usnewcustomers** to create
univ.mastercustomers. Be certain that the observations in the new SAS data set
are sorted in ascending **CustomerID** order.

1. Use PROC SORT to create temporary versions of **univ.uscustomers** and
   univ.usnewcustomers that are sorted according to **CustomerID**.

```
proc sort data=univ.uscustomers
          out=uscustomers;
   by CustomerID;
run;
proc sort data=univ.usnewcustomers
          out=usnewcustomers;
   by CustomerID;
run;
```

Partial SAS Log

```
10    proc sort data=univ.uscustomers
11            out=uscustomers;
12       by CustomerID;
13    run;

NOTE: There were 290 observations read from the data set UNIV.USCUSTOMERS.
NOTE: The data set WORK.USCUSTOMERS has 290 observations and 7 variables.
NOTE: PROCEDURE SORT used (Total process time):
      real time           0.04 seconds
      cpu time            0.05 seconds


14    proc sort data=univ.usnewcustomers
15            out=usnewcustomers;
16       by CustomerID;
17    run;

NOTE: There were 20 observations read from the data set UNIV.USNEWCUSTOMERS.
NOTE: The data set WORK.USNEWCUSTOMERS has 20 observations and 7 variables.
NOTE: PROCEDURE SORT used (Total process time):
      real time           0.43 seconds
      cpu time            0.04 seconds
```

2. Create **univ.mastercustomers** by interleaving **work.uscustomers** and
   work.usnewcustomers. Examine the new data set to verify that the observations were combined
   and sorted according to values of **CustomerID**.

Partial SAS Log

```
17    data univ.mastercustomers;
18       set uscustomers usnewcustomers;
19       by CustomerID;
20    run;

NOTE: There were 290 observations read from the data set WORK.USCUSTOMERS.
NOTE: There were 20 observations read from the data set WORK.USNEWCUSTOMERS.
NOTE: The data set UNIV.MASTERCUSTOMERS has 310 observations and 7 variables.
NOTE: DATA statement used (Total process time):
      real time           0.02 seconds
      cpu time            0.02 seconds
```

Partial SAS Output

```
        Customer  Customer  Customer
   Obs     ID     FirstName LastName    CustomerAddress        CustomerGroup

    1    000022   Rose      Buffardi    23 Creek Park Way      Orion Club Gold
    2    000492   David     Dulin       147 Bowling Farm Ct    Orion Club
    3    000551   Blu       Peachey     85 Lake Boone Trl      Internet/Catalog Customers
    4    000738   Jerry     Krejci      700 Fernwood Dr        Orion Club Gold
    5    000777   Franklyn  Deverger    310 Hemphill Dr        Orion Club
    6    000816   Kerr      Moorer      1 Lakeside Dr          Orion Club Gold
    7    001177   Fay       Upchurch    1736 Foliage Cir       Orion Club
    8    001379   Antwoine  Exelbierd   194 Chatham Ln         Orion Club Gold
    9    002232   Janice    Carter      232 Paige Road         Orion Club
   10    002347   Ava       Conner      2226 Hilburn Drive     Orion Club


   Obs   CustomerType       CustomerAddress2

    1    high activity      Lavallette, NJ 08735
    2    low activity       Tahlequah, OK 74464
    3                       Keysville, GA 30816
    4    medium activity    Minneapolis, MN 55436
    5    inactive           Honolulu, HI 96818
    6    medium activity    Auburn Hills, MI 48326
    7    medium activity    Starke, FL 32091
    8    high activity      Charleston, WV 25302
    9    inactive           Toronto, OH 43964
   10    medium activity    Arlington, TX 76013
```

 **Exercises**

1. Interleaving SAS Data Sets

Create the data set **work.allusemps** as the result of interleaving two data sets. Add a new variable named **GrpCode** for selected employee departments. Create a report using the new data set that displays the annual salaries of each employee group.

a. Use the SORT procedure to create temporary data sets of **univ.usemps** and **univ.newemps2002** that are sorted by **EmployeeID**.

b. Write a DATA step that creates **work.allusemps** by interleaving the sorted versions of **univ.usemps** and **univ.newemps2002** according to **EmployeeID**. Include only the Sales Management, Administration, and Engineering departments in the data set being created.

Use the following table to create a new variable named **GrpCode**:

EmployeeDepartment	EmployeeGroup	GroupCode
Sales Management	Sales Management	SMSM
Administration	Administration	ADAD
	Shipping Charges	ADSC
	Stock Admin	ADSA
	Security Guards	ADSG
	Service	ADSV
Engineering	Electrical Workshop	ENEW
	Engineering	ENEN

c. Use the PRINT procedure to verify the data was created properly.

Partial SAS Output

```
   Employee                              Employee                          Grp
     ID        JobTitle                  Department      EmployeeGroup      Code


   00120995   Office Administrator       Administration   Administration      ADAD
   00120996   Office Assistant           Administration   Administration      ADAD
   00120997   Shipping Administrator     Administration   Shipping Charges    ADSC
   00120999   Clerk                      Administration   Shipping Charges    ADSC
   00121000   Administration Manager     Administration   Shipping Charges    ADSC
   00121001   Warehouse Manager          Administration   Stock Admin         ADSA
   00121003   Warehouse Assistant        Administration   Stock Admin         ADSA
   00121004   Security Manager           Administration   Security Guards     ADSG
   00121008   Security Guard             Administration   Security Guards     ADSG
```

4.2 Match-Merging SAS Data Sets

Objectives

- Explain how to match-merge SAS data sets.
- Use the MERGE statement in a DATA step to combine SAS data sets.
- Use the IN= data set option to control nonmatches in merging.
- Use the RENAME= data set option when you merge SAS data sets.

20

Match-Merging

Match-merging

- combines observations from two or more SAS data sets into a single observation in a new data set according to the values of a common variable
- can be used to combine observations having a one-to-one, one-to-many, or many-to-many relationship.

21

Data Relationships

- In a one-to-one relationship, a single observation in one data set is related to a single observation in another data set.

- In a one-to-many relationship, unique observations in one data set are related to multiple observations in the second data set.

- In a many-to-many relationship, multiple observations in one data set may be related to multiple observations in another data set.

22

Business Scenario

The data set `univ.customerorders` contains sales order information.

Customer ID	Order Date	OrderID	ProductID	Quantity	Price
029858	15128	1239347234	230100600005	4	130
029858	15171	1239686972	240800100020	1	122
029858	15171	1239686972	240800100036	1	468

The `univ.mastercustomers` contains mailing address and other information about customers.

Customer ID	Customer FirstName	Customer LastName	CustomerAddress	CustomerGroup
000492	David	Dulin	147 Bowling Farm Ct	Orion Club
000551	Blu	Peachey	85 Lake Boone Trl	Internet/...
000738	Jerry	Krejci	700 Fernwood Dr	Orion Club Gold

23

Match-Merging

Create a data set named `shipping` that contains the name and addresses of customers who have placed orders by merging the `univ.customerorders` data set and the `univ.mastercustomers` data set.

Partial SAS Output

Customer ID	Order Date	...	Customer First Name	Customer LastName	CustomerAddress
029858	15128	...	Alice	Maxam	81 Flagstone Pl
029858	15171	...	Alice	Maxam	81 Flagstone Pl
029858	15171	...	Alice	Maxam	81 Flagstone Pl

24

Coding the Match-Merge

Data sets combined with a match-merge must be sorted by the common variable. Use PROC SORT to prepare data if necessary.

The DATA step with a MERGE statement and a BY statement is used to match-merge two or more SAS data sets.

General form of the DATA step:

```
DATA SAS-data-set ;
    MERGE SAS-data-set-1 SAS-data-set-2;
    BY variable(s);
RUN;
```

25

✐   All input data sets must be sorted or indexed by the variable(s) listed in the BY statement.

Match-Merging with Nonmatches

```
proc sort data=univ.customerorders
         out = customerorders;
   by CustomerID;


proc sort data=univ.mastercustomers
         out=mastercustomers;
   by CustomerID;


data shipping;
   merge customerorders
         mastercustomers ;
   by CustomerID;
run;
```

26   c04s2d1.sas

Match-Merging with Nonmatches

By default, SAS writes all observations, matches and
nonmatches, to the output data set.

Partial `customerorders`   Partial `mastercustomers`
data set   data set

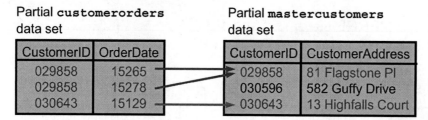

CustomerID	OrderDate
029858	15265
029858	15278
030643	15129

CustomerID	CustomerAddress
029858	81 Flagstone Pl
030596	582 Guffy Drive
030643	13 Highfalls Court

Partial `work.shipping` data set

CustomerID	OrderDate	CustomerAddress
029858	15265	81 Flagstone Pl
029858	15278	81 Flagstone Pl
030596	.	582 Guffy Drive
030643	15129	13 Highfalls Court

27   ...

Controlling Nonmatches

- The IN= data set option identifies whether a SAS data set contributed data to the PDV.
- An IF statement conditionally enables a following statement to execute.
- Combined use of the two techniques writes out only matches to the final data set.

28

The IN= Data Set Option

General form of the DATA step with the IN= data set option:

```
DATA SAS-data-set ;
    MERGE SAS-data-set-1 (IN=IN1)
            SAS-data-set-2 (IN=IN2);
    BY variable(s);
RUN;
```

29

The IN= option creates a temporary variable that indicates whether the data set contributed data to the current observation. The variable has a value of 1 when the data set contributed to the current observation. Otherwise it has a value of 0. The variable created by the IN= data set option is available for processing in the DATA step, but is not written to the output data set.

Eliminating Nonmatches

```
proc sort data=univ.customerorders
          out=customerorders;
   by CustomerID;
run;

proc sort data=univ.mastercustomers
          out=mastercustomers;
   by CustomerID;
run;

data shipping;
   merge customerorders (in=inorders)
         mastercustomers (in=inmaster);
   by CustomerID;
   if inorders=1 and inmaster=1;
run;
```

30   c04s2d2.sas

Eliminating Nonmatches

The observations that do **not** appear in **both** data sets
are **not** written to the new data set.

Partial `customerorders`   Partial `mastercustomers`
data set   data set

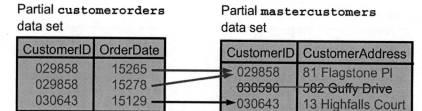

CustomerID	OrderDate
029858	15265
029858	15278
030643	15129

CustomerID	CustomerAddress
029858	81 Flagstone Pl
~~030596~~	~~582 Guffy Drive~~
030643	13 Highfalls Court

Partial `work.shipping` data set

CustomerID	OrderDate	CustomerAddress
029858	15265	81 Flagstone Pl
029858	15278	81 Flagstone Pl
030643	15129	13 Highfalls Court

31   ...

The RENAME= Data Set Option

The RENAME= data set option can be used to change the name of a variable from an input data set in the PDV.

General form of the RENAME= data set option:

> *SAS-data-set*(**RENAME** = (*old-name* = *new-name*))

32

✎   Use of the RENAME= data set option does not change how the variable name is stored in the original input data sets.

Using the RENAME= Option

If the key variable in the last example were named differently in each data set, then the RENAME= option would need to be used.

Partial Orders Information

CustNum	OrderDate
029858	15265
029858	15278
030643	15129

Partial Customer Information

CustomerID	CustomerAddress
029858	81 Flagstone Pl
030596	582 Guffy Drive
030643	13 Highfalls Court

33

Using the RENAME= Option

```
proc sort data=univ.customerorders
          out=customerorders;
   by CustomerID;
run;

proc sort data=univ.mastercustomers
          out=mastercustomers;
   by CustomerID;
run;

data shipping;
   merge customerorders ((in=inorders)
                 rename=(CustNum=CustomerID))
         mastercustomers (in=inmaster);
   by CustomerID;
   if inorders=1 and inmaster=1;
run;
```

34

Match-Merging in the DATA Step

c04s2d1.sas

The data set **univ.customerorders** contains sales order information. The data set
univ.mastercustomers contains mailing address and other information about customers. Both data
sets contain a **CustomerID** variable. Create a data set that contains the names and addresses of
customers who have placed orders.

1. Sort the input data sets by the common variable **CustomerID**.

```
proc sort data=univ.customerorders out=customerorders;
   by CustomerID;
run;
proc sort data=univ.mastercustomers out=mastercustomers;
   by CustomerID;
run;
```

2. Create a new data set named **shipping** by merging the **customerorders** data set with the
    mastercustomers data set according to **CustomerID** values. Use IN= variables to output only
    the observations that match. Create a new variable named **TotalSale** that calculates the total
    amount of each order based on the values of **Quantity** and **UnitPrice**.

```
data shipping;
   merge customerorders (in=inorders)
         mastercustomers (in=inmaster);
   by CustomerID;
   if inorders=1 and inmaster=1;
   TotalSale=Quantity*UnitPrice;
run;
```

3. Use the PRINT procedure to view the data portion of **shipping**.

```
proc print data=shipping;
run;
```

Partial SAS Output

Obs	Customer ID	Order Date	OrderID	ProductID	Quantity	Unit Price	Customer First Name	Customer LastName
1	029858	15128	1239347234	230100600005	4	130	Alice	Maxam
2	029858	15171	1239686972	240800100020	1	122	Alice	Maxam
3	029858	15171	1239686972	240800100036	1	468	Alice	Maxam

Obs	CustomerAddress	CustomerGroup	CustomerType	CustomerAddress2	Total Sale
1	81 Flagstone Pl	Orion Club Gold	medium activity	Bryans Road, MD 20616	520
2	81 Flagstone Pl	Orion Club Gold	medium activity	Bryans Road, MD 20616	122
3	81 Flagstone Pl	Orion Club Gold	medium activity	Bryans Road, MD 20616	468

Optional Demonstration

The Marketing Department wants to look at data to plan a marketing campaign. Use the **shipping** data set that was just created and the GCHART procedure to generate a report that displays the total amount of orders from each state.

1. Create a **marketing** data set that extracts the state values from address information stored in a variable named **Address2**.

```
data marketing;
   set shipping;
   State=substr(scan(CustomerAddress2,2,','),2,2);
run;
```

2. Use the GCHART procedure to display the results.

```
title 'Total Sales';
proc gchart data=marketing;
   vbar state / sumvar=TotalSale ;
run;
quit;
```

SAS Output

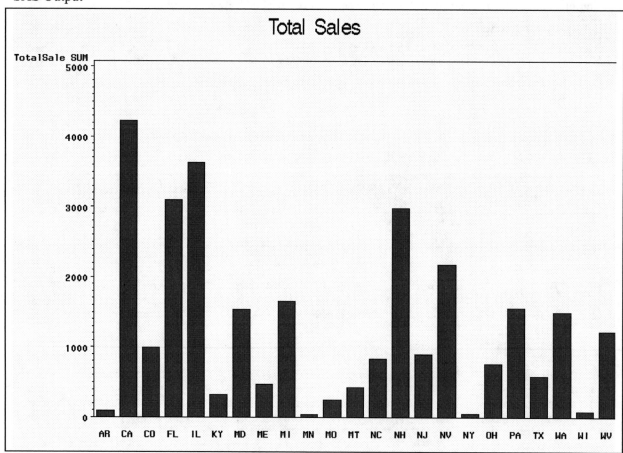

 **Exercises**

2. Merging SAS Data Sets

Write a DATA step to create **work.alltotsales** by combining **univ.totsales**, which contains sales information for each employee for the years 1999-2001, with a data set that contains the sales data for each employee for 2002 (**univ.totsales2002**). In the resulting data set, you will be adding a new variable for each observation.

a. Use PROC SORT to order the observations in **univ.totsales** and **univ.totsales2002** according to ascending values of the identification number of the employee. Note that the variable that contains the employee's ID has a different name in each data set. Save the sorted observations in temporary SAS data sets.

b. Create **work.alltotsales** by match-merging the sorted version of **univ.totsales** and the sorted version of **univ.totsales2002**.

c. Modify the previous DATA step that created **work.alltotsales**. Create a new variable **SalesTotals** that is the sum of the total sales from 1999 to 2002. The data set should only contain the variables **EmployeeID**, **EmployeeName**, **TotSales1999**, **TotSales2000**, **TotSales2001**, **TotSales2002**, and **SalesTotals**.

d. View the data portion of **work.alltotsales** with the PRINT procedure. Add a format statement to display the numeric variables with two decimal places.

Partial SAS Output

```
                            The SAS System

      Employee              Tot        Tot        Tot        Tot      Sales
Obs     ID      EmployeeName  Sales1999  Sales2000  Sales2001  Sales2002  Totals

  1   00121020  Cherda Ridley       1761.50    1497.50     163.30    3422.30   6844.60
  2   00121021  Priscilla Farren     104.90    2341.80      48.80    2495.50   4991.00
  3   00121024  Michael Westlund       0.00     227.20     534.70     761.90   1523.80
  4   00121025  Barnaby Cassey       617.00    1011.10    2516.30    4144.40   8288.80
  5   00121027  Allan Rudder          70.20     304.10     206.40     580.70   1161.40
  6   00121029  Kuo-Chung Mcelwee    118.60     540.40     340.40     999.40   1998.80
  7   00121030  Jeryl Areu           406.20      71.80     543.30    1021.30   2042.60
  8   00121031  Scott Filan          151.10     285.50     274.80     711.40   1422.80
  9   00121033  Kristie Snitzer        0.00     350.30     109.90     460.20    920.40
 10   00121035  James Blackley       254.98     483.80     676.60    1415.38   2830.76
 11   00121037  Muthukumar Miketa   1066.60     961.78    2195.00    4223.38   8446.76
 12   00121039  Donald Washington   1200.60     631.80    2722.50    4554.90   9109.80
```

4.3 Solutions to Exercises

1. Interleaving SAS Data Sets

```
proc sort data=univ.usemps out=work.usemps;
   by EmployeeID;
run;

proc sort data=univ.newemps2002 out=work.newemps2002;
   by EmployeeID;
run;

data work.allusemps;
   set work.usemps work.newemps2002;
   by EmployeeID;
   length GrpCode $ 4;
   if EmployeeDepartment in ('Sales Management',
                             'Administration',
                             'Engineering');

   if EmployeeDepartment='Sales Management' then GrpCode='SMSM';
   else if EmployeeDepartment='Administration' then do;
      if EmployeeGroup='Administration' then GrpCode='ADAD';
      else if EmployeeGroup='Shipping Charges' then
                     GrpCode='ADSC';
      else if EmployeeGroup='Stock Admin' then GrpCode='ADSA';
      else if EmployeeGroup='Security Guards' then GrpCode='ADSG';
      else if EmployeeGroup='Service' then GrpCode='ADSV';
   end;

   else if EmployeeDepartment='Engineering' then do;
      if EmployeeGroup='Electrical Workshop' then GrpCode='ENEW';
      else if EmployeeGroup='Engineering' then GrpCode='ENEN';
   end;
run;

proc print data=work.allusemps;
   var EmployeeID JobTitle EmployeeDepartment EmployeeGroup GrpCode;
run;
```

2. Merging SAS Data Sets

```
proc sort data=univ.totsales2002 out=work.totsales2002;
   by EmpID;
run;

proc sort data=univ.totsales out=work.totsales;
   by EmployeeID;
run;


data work.alltotsales
   merge work.totsales
         work.totsales2002(rename= (EmpId=EmployeeID));
   by EmployeeID;
run;

data work.alltotsales (keep=EmployeeID EmployeeName TotSales1999
                            TotSales2000 TotSales2001 TotSales2002
                            SalesTotals);
   merge work.totsales
         work.totsales2002(rename= (EmpID=EmployeeID));
   by EmployeeID;
   SalesTotals=sum(totsales1999, totsales2000, totsales2001,
     totsales2002 );
run;

proc print data=work.alltotsales;
   format TotSales1999 TotSales2000 TotSales2001
          Totsales2002 SalesTotals 8.2;
run;
```

Chapter 5   Accessing Data from Other Sources

5.1   Accessing a Microsoft Excel Workbook...5-3

5.2   Creating a SAS Data Set Using the Import Wizard (Self-Study) 5-16

5.3   Solutions to Exercises 5-27

5.1 Accessing a Microsoft Excel Workbook

Objectives

- Use the LIBNAME statement to specify options required to access a Microsoft Excel workbook.
- Merge a Microsoft Excel table with a SAS data set.

3

How to Access a Microsoft Excel Workbook

The LIBNAME statement enables you to do the following:

- assign a SAS libref directly to a Microsoft Excel workbook
- use options to specify connection information

4

Microsoft Excel LIBNAME Statement

General form of a Microsoft Excel LIBNAME statement:

LIBNAME *libref 'location-of-Excel-workbook' <options>*;

Example:

```
libname myxls 'c:\classes\enrollment.xls';
```

5

You must have SAS/ACCESS to PC Files licensed and installed to use the Microsoft Excel LIBNAME engine.

Microsoft Excel LIBNAME Statement Options

DBMAX_TEXT=*n*
indicates the length of the longest character string, where *n* is an integer between 256 and 32,767 inclusive. Any character string with a length greater than this value is truncated.

The default is 1024.

6

Microsoft Excel LIBNAME Statement Options

GETNAMES=YES | NO

> determines whether SAS will use the first row of data in a Microsoft Excel worksheet or range as column names.
>
> YES   specifies to use the first row of data in an Excel worksheet or range as column names.
>
> NO   specifies **not** to use the first row of data in an Excel worksheet or range as column names. SAS generates and uses the variable names F1, F2, F3, and so on.

The default is YES.

7

Microsoft Excel LIBNAME Statement Options

MIXED=YES | NO

> specifies whether to import data with both character and numeric values and convert all data to character.
>
> YES   specifies that all data values will be converted to character.
>
> NO   specifies that numeric data will be missing when a character type is assigned. Character data will be missing when a numeric data type is assigned.

The default is NO.

8

Microsoft Excel LIBNAME Statement Options

SCANTEXT=YES | NO

    specifies whether to read the entire data column and use the length of the longest string found as the SAS column width.

    YES scans the entire data column and uses the longest string value to determine the SAS column width.

    NO   does not scan the column and defaults to a width of 255.

The default is YES.

9

Microsoft Excel LIBNAME Statement Options

SCANTIME=YES | NO

    specifies whether to scan all row values in a date/time column and automatically determine the TIME data type if **only** time values exist.

    YES specifies that a column with only time values be assigned the TIME8. format.

    NO   specifies that a column with only time values be assigned the DATE9. format.

The default is NO.

10

The TIME8. format displays the time as *hh:mm:ss*, for example, 11:07:53.
The DATE9. format displays the date as *ddmmmyyyy*, for example, 18MAY2007.

Microsoft Excel LIBNAME Statement Options

USEDATE=YES | NO

> specifies whether to use the DATE9. format for date/time values in Excel workbooks.

> > YES specifies that date/time values be assigned the DATE9. format.

> > NO   specifies that date/time values be assigned the DATETIME16. format.

The default is YES.

11

The DATETIME. format displays the datetime as *ddmmmyy:hh:mm:ss.ss*, for example, 18MAY07:05:03:49:19

Microsoft Excel LIBNAME Statement

For demos and exercises, use the workbook **employees.xls**. It contains the following sheets:

- Employees
- NewEmps2002
- USEmps
- Managers
- Sheet1

The basic LIBNAME statement you use is as follows:

```
libname xlsdata 'employees.xls';
```

c05s1d1.sas

12

Issuing a LIBNAME Statement to Microsoft Excel Data

c05s1d2.sas

This demonstration illustrates how to submit a LIBNAME statement to connect to Microsoft Excel data.

1. Open Microsoft Excel to review the workbook employees.xls. Review the data in all the worksheets.

   Output for the Managers worksheet

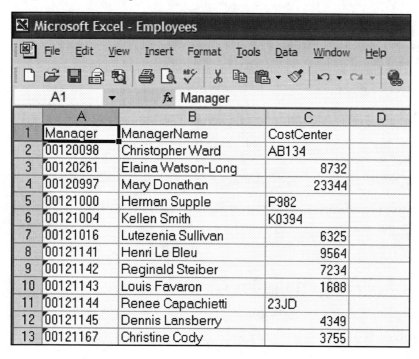

2. Close the worksheet.

3. If not already open, invoke SAS.

4. Submit the following LIBNAME statement to your Microsoft Excel workbook.

```
libname xlsdata 'employees.xls';
```

5. Check the log to verify the libref was successfully assigned.

```
1    libname xlsdata 'employees.xls';
NOTE: Libref XLSDATA was successfully assigned as follows:
      Engine:        EXCEL
      Physical Name: employees.xls
```

6. Use the SAS Explorer window to investigate the data sets in the Microsoft Excel library.
    select **Libraries** ⇨ **xlsdata**.

✎   Microsoft Excel follows its sheet names with a $. Names without the $ indicate a named range.

7. Double-click the **Managers$** data set. Why are some of the values for CostCenter missing?

⬛ VIEWTABLE: Xlsdata.Managers$			
	Manager	ManagerName	CostCenter
1	00120098	Christopher Ward	.
2	00120261	Elaina Watson-Long	8732
3	00120997	Mary Donathan	23344
4	00121000	Herman Supple	.
5	00121004	Kellen Smith	.
6	00121016	Lutezenia Sullivan	6325
7	00121141	Henri Le Bleu	9564
8	00121142	Reginald Steiber	7234
9	00121143	Louis Favaron	1688
10	00121144	Renee Capachietti	.
11	00121145	Dennis Lansberry	4349
12	00121167	Christine Cody	3755

8. Add the MIXED=YES option to the LIBNAME statement and submit the code.

```
libname xlsdata 'employees.xls' mixed=yes;
```

9. Navigate back to **Libraries** ⇨ **xlsdata**.

10. Open the Managers data set. Notice all CostCenters are included.

	Manager	ManagerName	CostCenter
1	00120098	Christopher Ward	AB134
2	00120261	Elaina Watson-Long	8732
3	00120997	Mary Donathan	23344
4	00121000	Herman Supple	P982
5	00121004	Kellen Smith	K0394
6	00121016	Lutezenia Sullivan	6325
7	00121141	Henri Le Bleu	9564
8	00121142	Reginald Steiber	7234
9	00121143	Louis Favaron	1688
10	00121144	Renee Capachietti	23JD
11	00121145	Dennis Lansberry	4349
12	00121167	Christine Cody	3755

VIEWTABLE: XIsdata.Managers$

11. Close the **Managers$** data set.

Working with the Microsoft Excel Data

After the LIBNAME statement is issued successfully, treat the Excel workbook as the SAS data library and the worksheets as the data sets.

All worksheets will be referenced as a typical SAS data set, that is, *libref.data-set-name*. If the sheet name contains special characters, you must use the SAS name literal construct of *libref*."sheet1$"n.

14

The CONTENTS Procedure

Use the CONTENTS procedure to obtain a list of variables and their attributes within a data set.

General form of the CONTENTS procedure:

```
PROC CONTENTS DATA=libref.data-set-name;
RUN;
```

15

continued...

The CONTENTS Procedure

Example:

```
proc contents data=xlsdata."Managers$"n;
run;
```

Partial Output

```
          Alphabetic List of Variables and Attributes

   #   Variable      Type   Len   Format   Informat   Label

   3   CostCenter    Char    5    $5.      $5.        CostCenter
   1   ManagerName   Char    8    $8.      $8.        ManagerName
   2   Manager       Char   18    $18.     $18.       Manager
```

16   c05s1d3.sas

The CONTENTS Procedure

Example:

```
proc contents data=univ.employees;
run;
```

Partial Output

```
  Alphabetic List of Variables and Attributes

     #    Variable     Type    Len

    10    Bonus        Num      8
    ...   ...          ...      ...
     6    Manager      Char     8
     2    Name         Char    20
     7    Salary       Num      8
     9    YearsOnJob   Num      8
```

17   c05s1d3.sas

The PRINT Procedure

To display the data values in the data set, use the PRINT procedure.

```
proc print data=xlsdata."Managers$"n;
run;
```

Partial Output

```
                      The SAS System

                                            Cost
     Obs    Manager    ManagerName          Center

      1     00120098   Christopher Ward     AB134
      2     00120261   Elaina Watson-Long   8732
      3     00120997   Mary Donathan        23344
      4     00121000   Herman Supple        P982
      5     00121004   Kellen Smith         K0394
```

c05s1d4.sas

18

The PRINT Procedure

To display the data values in the data set, use the PRINT procedure.

```
proc print data=univ.employees;
run;
```

Partial Output

```
                      The SAS System

                              Hire    Years
     Obs    Manager    Salary  Date    OnJob    Bonus

      1     00121143   22710   9862     14      2080
      2     00121145   25110  10105     14      2150
      3     00121143   25125   6179     24      3150
      4     00121144   25660   4230     30      3770
```

c05s1d4.sas

19

Merging a SAS Data Set and Excel Worksheet

Merge two data sets to find the manager name for each employee. The manager name is in the Excel worksheet **Managers** and the employee name is in the **Employees** SAS data set.

```
data work.newdemo(keep=Name ManagerName
                       CostCenter);
   merge xlsdata."managers$"n(in=m)
         work.employees(in=e);
   by manager;
   if m and e;
run;
proc print data=work.newdemo;
   var Name ManagerName CostCenter;
run;
```

20   c05s1d5.sas

    This example returns managers who have employees.

Merging a SAS Data Set and Excel Worksheet

Partial Output

```
                      The SAS System

                                               Cost
   Obs    Name                  ManagerName    Center

    1    Henri Le Bleu          Elaina Watson-Long  8732
    2    Sherelyn Heilmann      Mary Donathan       23344
    3    Mary Donathan          Herman Supple       P982
    4    Kellen Smith           Herman Supple       P982
    5    Johannes Wade          Herman Supple       P982
    6    Robert Goodwin         Herman Supple       P982
    7    Tony House             Herman Supple       P982
    8    Lutezenia Sullivan     Herman Supple       P982
    9    Eron Mckenzie          Kellen Smith        K0394
```

21

Working with the Microsoft Excel Data

c05s1d6.sas

Use a DATA step to match-merge **xlsdata.managers$** with **univ.employees** according to the values of **manager**. Display the results.

1. Use the CONTENTS procedure to examine the descriptor portion of **xlsdata.managers$**.

```
proc contents data=xlsdata."managers$"n;
run;
```

2. Use the CONTENTS procedure to examine the descriptor portion of **univ.employees**.

```
proc contents data=univ.employees;
run;
```

3. Create **work.newdemo** by merging **xlsdata.managers$** and **work.employees** (the sorted version of **univ.employees**) according to **manager**. Keep the variables **Name**, **ManagerName**, and **CostCenter**. Examine the data portion of the new data set.

```
proc sort data=univ.employees out=work.employees;
    by manager;
run;

data work.newdemo(keep=Name ManagerName CostCenter);
    merge xlsdata."managers$"n(in=m)
          work.employees(in=e);
    by manager;
    if m and e;
run;

proc print data=work.newdemo;
    var Name ManagerName CostCenter;
run;
```

Partial SAS Output

```
                               The SAS System

                                                       Cost
            Obs     Name                ManagerName    Center

              1     Henri Le Bleu       Elaina Watson-Long   8732
              2     Sherelyn Heilmann   Mary Donathan        23344
              3     Mary Donathan       Herman Supple        P982
              4     Kellen Smith        Herman Supple        P982
              5     Johannes Wade       Herman Supple        P982
              6     Robert Goodwin      Herman Supple        P982
              7     Tony House          Herman Supple        P982
              8     Lutezenia Sullivan  Herman Supple        P982
              9     Eron Mckenzie       Kellen Smith         K0394
```

5.2 Creating a SAS Data Set Using the Import Wizard (Self-Study)

Objectives

- Use the Import Wizard to create a SAS data set from a comma-separated text file.

24

What Is the Import Wizard?

The *Import Wizard* is a point-and-click graphical interface that enables you to create a SAS data set from several types of external files including the following:

- dBASE files (*.DBF)
- Excel spreadsheets (*.XLS)
- Microsoft Access tables (.MDB)
- delimited files (*.*)
- comma-separated values (*.CSV)
- JMP files (*.JMP)

25

The data sources available to you depend on the SAS/ACCESS products that you license. If you do not have any licensed SAS/ACCESS products, the only types of data source files available to you are

- .CSV
- .TXT
- delimited files (such as tab, space, and |)

Using the Import Wizard to Create a SAS Data Set

Use the Import Wizard to import the file **demotrades.csv** into SAS. This is a comma-delimited file that contains information on trades. Name the resulting data set **work.trades**.

1. Select **File** ⇨ **Import Data...**. The Import Wizard – Select import type window opens.

2. Select the drop-down button to select a data source.

3. From the list box, select **Comma Separated Values (*.csv)**.

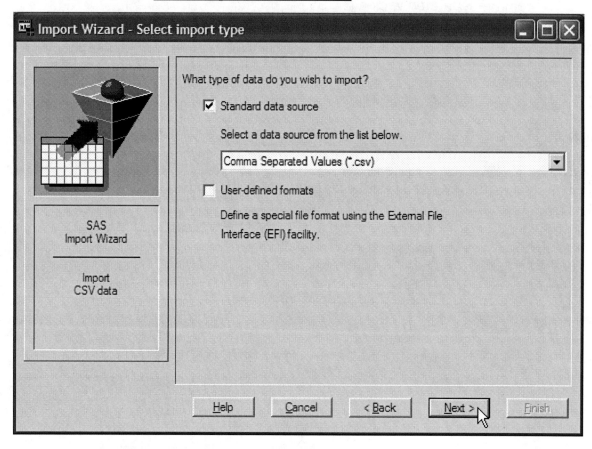

4. Select **Next**. The Import Wizard – Select file window opens.

5. Select **Browse**.

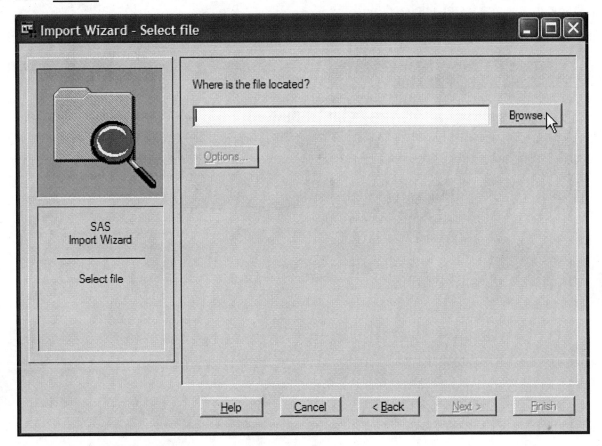

6. Navigate to **demotrades.csv** and select **Open**.

7. Select **Options...** to browse the available import options.

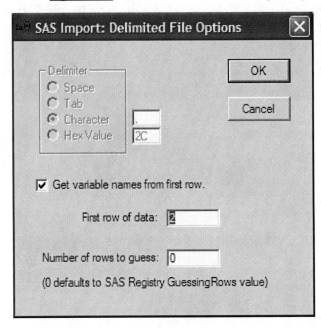

8. Select **OK** to accept the default values and close the window.

9. Select **Next** to open the Import Wizard – Select library and member window, where you specify the storage location for the imported file.

10. In the Library field, retain the library value as **WORK**. In the Member field, type **trades**.

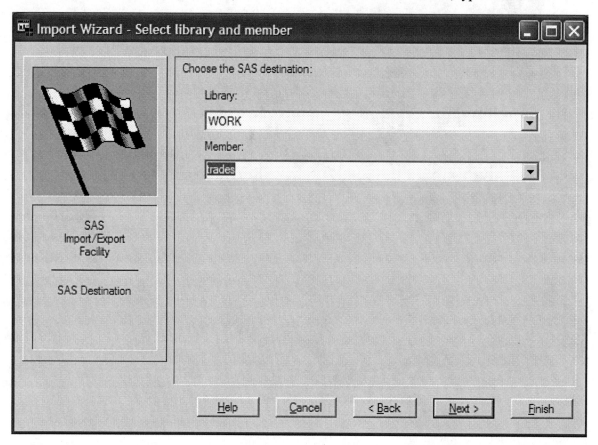

You can also select the pull-down arrow in the Library field and select a different library. You can select the pull-down arrow in the Member field and select an existing data set. If you select an existing data set, you are asked to verify that you want to replace it.

11. Select **Next** to move to the next window or **Finish** to create the SAS data set from the comma-delimited file.

    If you select **Finish** and you select the name of an existing SAS data set for the name of your new SAS data set (in the Import Wizard – Select library and member window), you are prompted to determine whether or not you want to replace the existing data set. Select **OK** or **Cancel**.

    If you select **Next**, the Import Wizard – Create SAS Statements window opens.

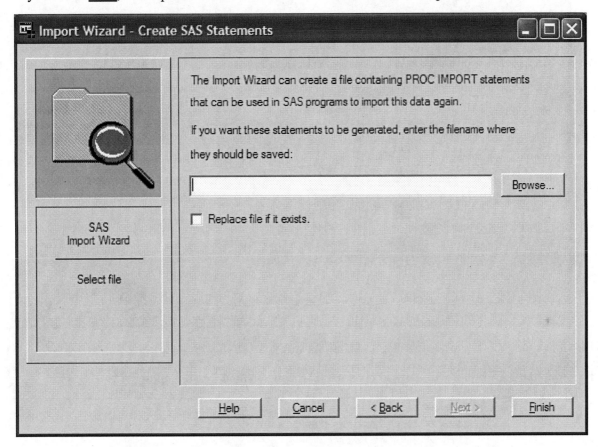

12. Type **importcode.sas**, which is the name of the file where you store the SAS code.

    You can also select **Browse...** to specify a location from the Save As window. After you select the pathname, select **Save** to complete your selections and return to the Import Wizard – Create SAS Statements window.

    If the file already exists, you are prompted to replace the existing file, append to the existing file, or cancel the save.

13. Select **Finish**.

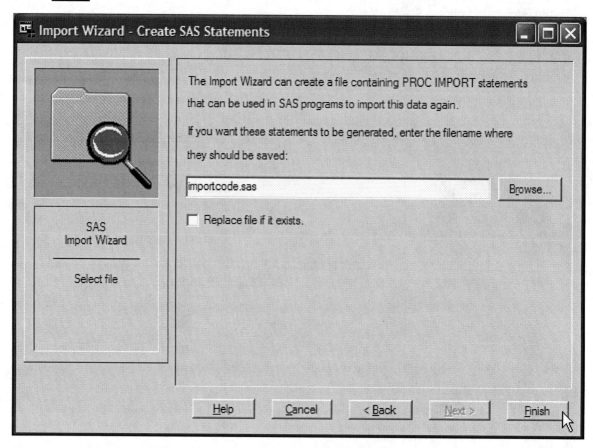

14. Check the SAS log to see that the SAS data set was successfully created.

15. Go to the SAS Editor window and open the SAS code created by the Import Wizard.

```
proc import out=work.trades
            datafile="demotrades.csv"
            dbms=csv replace;
   getnames=yes;
   datarow=2;
run;
```

The IMPORT Procedure

General form of the IMPORT procedure code that
is generated by the Import Wizard:

```
PROC IMPORT OUT=SAS-data-set
       DATAFILE='external-file-name'
       DBMS=file-type;
RUN;
```

27

The IMPORT procedure is a method for reading data from an external data source and writing it to a SAS data set.

DATAFILE='external-file-name'
                    specifies the complete path and filename of the input PC file, spreadsheet, or delimited external file.

OUT=SAS-data-set   identifies the output SAS data set with either a one- or a two-level SAS name (library and member name).

DBMS=file-type   specifies the type of data to import.

Available DBMS Specifications

Identifier	Input Data Source	Extension
ACCESS	Microsoft Access 2000, 2002, or 2003 table	.MDB
ACCESS97	Microsoft Access 97 table	.MDB
ACCESS2000	Microsoft Access 2000 table	.MDB
ACCESS2002	Microsoft Access 2002 table	.MDB
CSV	delimited file (comma-separated values)	.CSV
DBF	dBASE 5.0, IV, III+ and III files	.DBF
DLM	delimited file (default delimiter is a blank)	.*
EXCEL	Excel 2000, 2002, or 2003 spreadsheet	.XLS
EXCEL4	Excel 4.0 spreadsheet	.XLS
EXCEL5	Excel 5.0 or 95 spreadsheet	.XLS
EXCEL97	Excel 97 or 95 spreadsheet	.XLS
EXCEL2000	Excel 2000 spreadsheet	.XLS
JMP	JMP table	.JMP
TAB	delimited file (tab-delimited values)	.*
WK1	Lotus 1-2-3 Release 2 spreadsheet	.WK1
WK3	Lotus 1-2-3 Release 3 spreadsheet	.WK3
WK4	Lotus 1-2-3 Release 4 or 5 spreadsheet	.WK4

For more information on the options for the different data sources, please refer to the online documentation at http://support.sas.com/onlinedoc/913/getDoc/en/proc.hlp/a000312413.htm.

The IMPORT Procedure

Code that is generated by the Import Wizard when importing a comma-separated text file:

```
PROC IMPORT OUT=WORK.NEW
            DATAFILE="demotrades.csv"
            DBMS=CSV REPLACE;
    GETNAMES=YES;
    DATAROW=2;
RUN;
```

28

c05s2d1.sas

Exercises

1. **Issuing a Libref to a Microsoft Excel Workbook**

    a. Submit a LIBNAME statement to the Microsoft Excel workbook **employees.xls**. Use **xlsdata** as the library reference (libref) and any necessary options.

    b. Use the CONTENTS procedure to investigate the Microsoft Excel worksheet called **NewEmps2002$**.

    c. Create a new data set named **work.bonus2002** from **xlsdata.NewEmps2002$**. Create a column called **Bonus** that is 10% of the employee's **Salary**.

    d. Use the PRINT procedure to display the fields **EmployeeName**, **EmployeeDepartment**, **EmployeeHireDate**, and **Bonus**. Format **Bonus** with dollar signs and no decimal places.

    Desired output

    ```
                                  The SAS System

                                 Employee        Employee
          Obs    EmployeeName          Department      HireDate      Bonus

           1     Lily-Ann Gordo        Administration  01AUG2002     $3,485
           2     Troyce Van Der Wiele  Administration  01JUL2002     $2,600
           3     Terrill Jaime         Sales           01APR2002     $3,152
           4     Nasim Smith           Sales           01MAR2002     $3,134
           5     Richard Fay           Sales           01NOV2002     $2,690
           6     Clement Davis         Sales           01AUG2002     $3,019
           7     Debra Armant          Sales           01AUG2002     $3,031
           8     Corneille Malta       Sales           01APR2002     $2,804
           9     Agnieszka Holthouse   Sales           01FEB2002     $2,939
          10     Bryce Smotherly       Sales           01OCT2002     $2,859
          11     Rocheal Flammia       Sales           01JUN2002     $2,712
          12     Brian Farnsworth      Sales           01SEP2002     $2,726
          13     Rose Anger            Sales           01JUL2002     $3,138
    ```

2. **Reading a Comma-Delimited File (Optional)**

    a. Use the Import Wizard to create a SAS data set named **work.weather2** from the comma-delimited file **weather2.csv**.

    b. Use the CONTENTS procedure to display the descriptor portion of the SAS data set **work.weather2**.

    c. Use the PRINT procedure to display the data portion of the SAS data set **work.weather2**.

5.3 Solutions to Exercises

1. **Issuing a Libref to a Microsoft Excel Workbook**

   a.
   ```
   libname xlsdata 'employees.xls' mixed=yes;
   ```

   b.
   ```
   proc contents data=xlsdata."NewEmps2002$"n;
   run;
   ```

   c.
   ```
   data work.bonus2002;
      set xlsdata."NewEmps2002$"n;
      Bonus=salary*.10;
   run;
   ```

   d.
   ```
   proc print data=work.bonus2002;
      var EmployeeName EmployeeDepartment EmployeeHireDate Bonus;
      format Bonus dollar7.;
   run;
   ```

2. **Reading a Comma-delimited File**

   a. Use the Import Wizard to create a SAS data set named **work.weather2**.

      1) Select **File** ⇨ **Import Data…**.

      2) Select **Comma Separated Values (*.csv)** and select **Next**.

      3) Select **Browse** and navigate to **weather2.csv**.

      4) Select **Open** to select the file and select **Next**.

      5) Type **weather2** as the member and select **Next**.

      6) Select **Finish** to create the data set.

   b.
   ```
   proc contents data=work.weather2;
   run;
   ```

   c.
   ```
   proc print data=work.weather2;
   run;
   ```

Chapter 6   Creating and Using Macro Variables

6.1   Introduction to Macro Processing 6-3

6.2   Automatic Macro Variables...6-14

6.3   User-Defined Macro Variables...6-22

6.4   Solutions to Exercises 6-32

6.1 Introduction to Macro Processing

Objectives

- Identify different applications of the SAS macro facility.
- Learn where macro variables are stored.
- Substitute the value of a macro variable anywhere in a program.
- Monitor the value that is substituted when a macro variable is referenced.
- Display macro variable values and text in the SAS log.

3

Purpose of the Macro Facility

Using the macro language, you can write SAS programs that are dynamic, or capable of self-modification.

Specifically, the macro language enables you to

- create and resolve macro variables anywhere in a SAS program
- write special programs (macros) that generate tailored SAS code.

4

Essentially, the SAS macro facility is a text handler. The programmer associates text with a macro reference and the macro facility inserts the text dynamically, which enables the programmer to build flexible SAS programs.

This chapter focuses on the use of macro variables, but possible uses of macro programs are also presented in this section.

Displaying System Information

Using the macro language, you can utilize automatic macro variables that contain information regarding your system environment.

For example, some of these variables contain the

- date and time of the SAS session
- version of SAS software
- operating system.

5

Displaying System Information

```
               Sales for 2001 for Orion Star US Employees

Manager ID     Group             EmployeeID        Sales for 2001
00121143       GOLF              00121051            $1,061.00
               INDOOR SPORTS     00121053              $237.00
                                 00121054              $155.00
               RACKET SPORTS     00121081              $146.00
                                 00121082              $631.00


                         ①        ②         ③

               Report created 13:14 Thursday, 08APR04
                  on the WIN System using SAS 9.1
                         ④                  ⑤
```

① time of day   ④ operating system

② day of week   ⑤ release of SAS software

③ date (day, month, and year)

6

Substitute Information Multiple Times

The macro facility can substitute the same user-defined information into multiple locations within a single program.

Example: Substitute a numeric month of interest into multiple locations in a program.

```
proc print data=univ.CustomerOrders;
   where month(OrderDate)=Month-of-Interest;
   title 'Order Summary for';
   title2 'Month Number Month-of-Interest';
run;
```

7

Conditional Processing

The macro facility controls whether certain portions of a SAS program are processed based on specific conditions.

Example: Generate the detailed orders report on a daily basis, but generate the revenue summary report only on Friday.

8

Repetitive Processing

The macro facility generates portions of a SAS program repetitively and makes each iteration perform differently.

Example: Generate the same summary report for each year between 2000 and 2002.

9

Data-Driven Applications

The macro facility can be used to create programs that are data driven.

The SAS program can decide dynamically what changes need to be made to the program and generate the appropriate SAS statements automatically.

10

Tips on Writing Macro-Based Programs

If a macro-based program is used to generate SAS code,

- write and debug the desired SAS program without any macro coding
- be certain that the SAS program runs with hard-coded programming constants on a fixed set of data.

11

Global Macro Variables

When SAS is invoked, a global symbol table is created and initialized with automatic or system-defined macro variables.

You can also create *user-defined* global macro variables with the %LET statement:

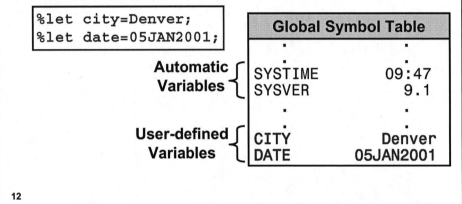

```
%let city=Denver;
%let date=05JAN2001;
```

Global Symbol Table	
.	.
.	.
.	.
SYSTIME	09:47
SYSVER	9.1
.	.
.	.
CITY	Denver
DATE	05JAN2001

Automatic Variables { SYSTIME / SYSVER

User-defined Variables { CITY / DATE

12

All macro variables are characters. Therefore, character strings or literals do not have to be enclosed in quotation marks. All characters between the equal sign and the semicolon are stored as part of the macro variable. Therefore, if the character string is enclosed in quotation marks, the quotation marks are stored as part of the value of the macro variable.

Referencing a Macro Variable

To substitute the value of a macro variable in your program, you must reference it.

A macro variable reference

- is made by preceding the macro variable name with an ampersand (&)
- causes the macro processor to search for the named macro variable and return its value from the symbol table if the variable exists.

13

Referencing a Macro Variable

Global Symbol Table	
CITY	Denver
DATE	05JAN2001

Example: Use a macro variable reference to make a substitution in a SAS program statement.

```
where OrderCity="&city";
```

generates

```
WHERE ORDERCITY="Denver";
```

14

If you need the resolved value of the macro variable to be enclosed in quotation marks, enclose the macro reference in double quotation marks in the code.

```
where cityst CONTAINS "&city";
```

The WHERE statement above generates

```
WHERE CITYST CONTAINS "Denver";
```

Macro variables enclosed in single quotation marks will not be resolved correctly.

```
where cityst CONTAINS '&city';
```

The WHERE statement above generates

```
WHERE CITYST CONTAINS '&city';
```

Referencing a Macro Variable

When the macro processor cannot act upon a macro variable reference, a message is printed in the SAS log.

Global Symbol Table	
CITY	Denver
DATE	05JAN2001

Referencing a nonexistent macro variable results in a warning message.

```
title "Orders from &cityst";
```

generates

```
WARNING: Apparent symbolic reference CITYST not resolved.
```

15

Referencing a Macro Variable

Global Symbol Table	
CITY	Denver
DATE	05JAN2001

Referencing an invalid macro variable name results in an error message.

```
title "Orders from &THE_CITY_IN_WHICH_THE_ORDER_ORIGINATED";
```

generates

```
ERROR: Symbolic variable name
       THE_CITY_IN_WHICH_THE_ORDER_ORIGINATED
       must be 32 or fewer characters long.
```

16

The name of a macro variable cannot exceed 32 characters in SAS®9.

Displaying Macro Variable Values

Use the SYMBOLGEN system option to monitor the value that is substituted for a macro variable referenced.

General form of the SYMBOLGEN system option:

OPTIONS SYMBOLGEN;

This system option displays the results of resolving macro variable references in the SAS log.

✎   The default option setting is NOSYMBOLGEN.

17

Displaying Macro Variable Values

Global Symbol Table	
CITY	Denver
DATE	05JAN2001

Partial SAS Log

```
where CustomerAddress2 contains "&city";
SYMBOLGEN: Macro variable CITY resolves to Denver
where CustomerAddress2 contains '&city';
```

Why is no message displayed for the final example?

18

Displaying Macro Variable Values

To verify the values of macro variables, you may want to write your own messages to the SAS log. The %PUT statement writes text to the SAS log.

General form of the %PUT statement:

%PUT *text* ;

19

Displaying Macro Variable Values

The %PUT statement

- writes to the SAS log only
- always writes to a new log line starting in column one
- writes a blank line if *text* is not specified
- does not require quotation marks around *text*
- resolves references to macro variables in *text* before *text* is written

20

continued...

Displaying Macro Variable Values

- removes leading and trailing blanks from *text* unless a macro quoting function is used
- wraps lines when the length of *text* is greater than the current line size setting
- can be used inside or outside a macro definition.

21

Displaying Macro Variable Values

Example: Write a message to the SAS log to verify
the value of the macro variable **CITY**.

Global Symbol Table	
CITY	Denver
DATE	05JAN2001

Partial SAS Log

```
%put The value of the macro variable CITY is: &city;
The value of the macro variable CITY is: Denver
```

22

6.2 Automatic Macro Variables

Objectives

- Identify selected automatic macro variables.
- Display values of automatic macro variables in the SAS log.

24

System-Defined Automatic Macro Variables

These variables
- are created at SAS invocation
- are global (always available)
- are usually assigned values by SAS
- can be assigned values by the user, in some cases.

25

System-Defined Automatic Macro Variables

Some automatic macro variables have fixed values that are set at SAS invocation:

Name	Value
SYSDATE	date of SAS invocation (DATE7.)
SYSDATE9	date of SAS invocation (DATE9.)
SYSDAY	day of the week of SAS invocation
SYSTIME	time of SAS invocation
SYSENV	FORE (interactive execution) BACK (noninteractive or batch execution)
SYSSCP	abbreviation for the operating system used such as OpenVMS, WIN, HP 300
SYSVER	release of SAS software being used
SYSJOBID	identifier of current SAS session or batch job mainframe systems: the userid or job name other systems: the process ID (PID)

26

System-Defined Automatic Macro Variables

Some automatic macro variables have values that change automatically, based on submitted SAS statements:

Name	Value
SYSLAST	name of the most recently created SAS data set in the form libref.name. If no data set was created, the value is _NULL_.
SYSPARM	text specified at program invocation.

27

System-Defined Automatic Macro Variables

Example: Substitute system information in footnotes
          for a report.

```
title 'Sales for 2001 for Orion Star US Employees';
footnote1 "This report was created in a SAS &sysver
session";
footnote2 "dated &sysdate9 (&systime)";

proc gchart data=sales3yrs;
   vbar EmployeeManager/sumvar=TotSales2001
                     type=sum;
   label EmployeeManager='Manager'
        TotSales2001='Total 2001 Sales';
   format TotSales2001 dollar9.;
run;
quit;
```

28   c06s2d1.sas

System-Defined Automatic Macro Variables

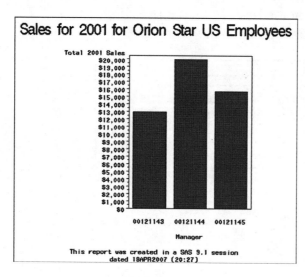

29

Displaying Automatic Macro Variables

The values of automatic macro variables can be displayed in the SAS log by specifying the _AUTOMATIC_ argument in the %PUT statement.

> **%PUT** _AUTOMATIC_;

30

Displaying Automatic Macro Variables

Partial SAS Log

The values of the macro variables **SYSDATE**,

SYSDATE9, and **SYSTIME** are character strings,

not SAS date or time values.

31

Applications for Automatic Variables

Possible applications for automatic macro variables:

SYSDATE or SYSDATE9	Check the current date to execute programs or on certain days of the month. Substitute the value in a TITLE statement.
SYSDAY	Check the value to run a given job on a certain day of the week.
SYSENV	Check the execution mode before submitting code that requires interactive (foreground) processing.

32

continued...

Applications for Automatic Variables

SYSVER	Check for the release of SAS software being used before executing a job with newer features.
SYSJOBID	Check who is currently executing the job to restrict certain processing or to issue commands specific to a user.
SYSERR	Check the return code from a SAS procedure or DATA step and abort the job if the return code is nonzero.
SYSRC	Check the return code of any system command before continuing with the job.

33

continued...

Applications for Automatic Variables

SYSLIBRC	Check the return code from a LIBNAME statement before attempting to access permanent SAS data sets.
SYSFILRC	Check the return code from a FILENAME statement before attempting to access a file other than a SAS file.
SYSSCP	Check the operating system in order to execute appropriate system commands.

34

Using SAS Automatic Macro Variables

c06s2d1.sas

Create a vertical bar chart that displays the **Sales3yrs** data for total sales in 2001 for each manager. Include a footnote that indicates system information automatically.

1. If the **Sales3yrs** data set is not in your work library, you will need to create it by opening a program named sales3yrs.sas in the **univ** library and submitting the program.

2. Verify that the following PROC step generates a vertical bar chart. Note that the date, time, and version of the SAS session are included in a footnote, so they are static values. To change them to the current date and time, you have to change the footnote each time that you run the program.

```
title 'Sales for 2001 for Orion Star US Employees';
footnote1 "This report was created in a SAS 9.1 session";
footnote2 "dated April 18, 2007 (20:27)";
proc gchart data=sales3yrs;
    vbar EmployeeManager/sumvar=TotSales2001
                         type=sum;
    label EmployeeManager='Manager' TotSales2001='Total 2001 Sales';
    format TotSales2001 dollar9.;
run;
quit;
```

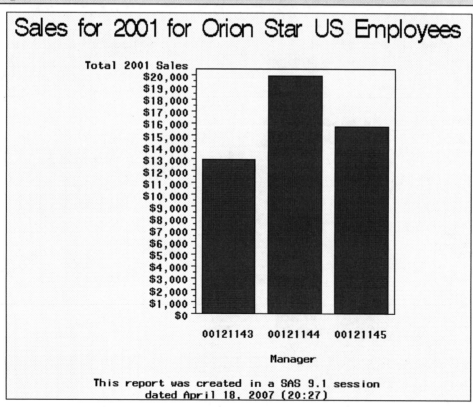

3. Use a %PUT statement to view the values of all automatic macro variables in the SAS log.

```
%put _automatic_;
```

Partial SAS Log

```
77  %put _automatic_;
AUTOMATIC AFDSID O
AUTOMATIC AFDSNAME
AUTOMATIC AFLIB
AUTOMATIC AFSTR1
AUTOMATIC AFSTR2
```

4. Modify the FOOTNOTE statement in the PROC step to automatically include the values of the **SYSVER**, **SYSDATE9**, and **SYSTIME** macro variables.

```
title 'Sales for 2001 for Orion Star US Employees';
footnote1 "This report was created in a SAS &sysver session";
footnote2 "dated &sysdate9 (&systime)";
proc gchart data=sales3yrs;
    vbar EmployeeManager/sumvar=TotSales2001
                        type=sum;
    label EmployeeManager='Manager' TotSales2001='Total 2001 Sales';
    format TotSales2001 dollar9.;
run;
quit;
```

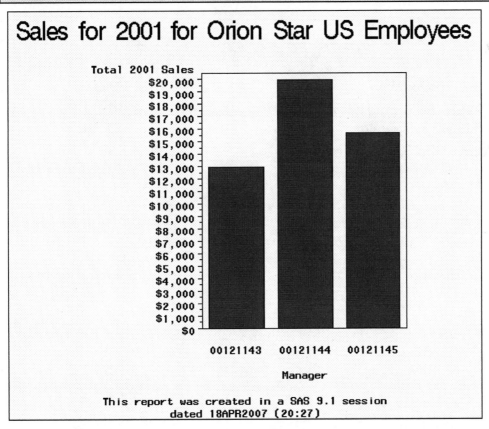

Your system, date, and time may differ from the footnote in this output.

6.3 User-Defined Macro Variables

Objectives

- Create user-generated macro variables.
- Display values of user-defined macro variables in the SAS log.

37

The %LET Statement

The %LET statement enables you to define a macro variable and assign it a value.

General form of the %LET statement:

```
%LET variable=value;
```

38

The %LET Statement

Rules for the %LET statement:

- *Variable* can be any name following the SAS naming convention.
- *Value* can be any string.
- If *variable* already exists in the symbol table, *value* **replaces** the current value.
- If either *variable* or *value* contains a macro statement or macro variable reference, the trigger is evaluated **before** the assignment is made.

39

continued...

The %LET Statement

Rules for the %LET statement:

- The maximum length is 64K characters.
- The minimum length is 0 characters (*null value*).
- Numeric tokens are stored as character strings.
- Mathematical expressions are **not** evaluated.
- The case of *value* is preserved.
- Quotes bounding literals are stored as part of *value*.
- Leading and trailing blanks **are removed** from *value* before the assignment is made.

40

A user-defined macro variable can be used to point to the location of files:

```
%let UNIV_Data=c:\workshop\winsas\hecpes;
```

Because symbol tables are stored in memory, consider resetting macro variables to null if they are no longer referenced, especially those with long values. For example, to change the length of the macro variable **CITY**, submit the following code:

```
%let city=;
```

 A macro variable can be deleted with the %SYMDEL statement as shown in the following code:

```
&SYMDEL city;
```

%LET Statement Examples

Use the rules on the previous page to determine the values assigned to macro variables by these %LET statements:

	Value
`%let name=Ed Norton;`	`Ed Norton`
`%let name2=' Ed Norton ';`	`' Ed Norton '`
`%let title="Joan's Report";`	`"Joan's Report"`
`%let start=;`	
`%let total=0;`	`0`
`%let sum=3+4;`	`3+4`
`%let total=&total+&sum;`	`0+3+4`
`%let x=varlist;`	`varlist`

49

%LET Statement Examples

Example: Assign the value **00121143** to the macro variable **MANAGER**. Use the macro variable to control program output.

```
%let Manager = 00121143;
title "2001 Sales for teams under Manager &manager";
footnote "Report created in a SAS &sysver session";
footnote2 "dated &sysdate (&systime)";
proc print data=sales3yrs label;
   var EmployeeName EmployeeID TotSales2001;
   label EmployeeName='Name'
         EmployeeID='ID'
         TotSales2001='Sales for 2001';
where EmployeeManager = "&manager";
run;
```

c06s3d1.sas

50

%LET Statement Examples

Partial SAS Output

```
       2001 Sales for teams under Manager 00121143

                                                  Sales
   Obs     Name                       ID        for 2001

    3      Elizabeth Spofford      00121060        1509
    6      John-Michael Plybon     00121086         252
    8      Tywanna Mcdade          00121053         237
   12      Susie Knudson           00121081         146
   13      Tzue-Ing Cormell        00121100           0
   14      Daniel Pulliam          00121054         155
```

51

Displaying User-Defined Macro Variables

The values of user-defined macro variables can be displayed in the SAS log by specifying the _USER_ argument in the %PUT statement.

```
%let Manager=00121143;
%put _user_;
```

52

continued...

Displaying User-Defined Macro Variables

Partial SAS Log

```
93  %let Manager = 00121143;

94  %put _user_;

GLOBAL MANAGER 0012114316
```

✎ The statement %put _all_; displays both automatic and user-defined macro variables.

53

Creating User-Defined Macro Variables

c06s3d1.sas

Create a list report showing **Sales3yrs** data for a particular manager.

1. Use a %LET statement to assign the value 00121143 to **Manager**. Use PROC REPORT to
    generate a list report. Write a WHERE statement that uses the macro variable **Manager** to select
    observations and a TITLE statement that references the value of **Manager**.

```
%let Manager = 00121143;

title "2001 Sales for teams under Manager &manager";
footnote "Report created in a SAS &sysver session";
footnote2 "dated &sysdate (&systime)";

proc print data=sales3yrs label;
   var EmployeeName EmployeeID TotSales2001;
   label EmployeeName='Name'
         EmployeeID='ID'
         TotSales2001='Sales for 2001';
   format TotSales2001 dollar9.;
   where EmployeeManager = "&manager";
run;
```

Partial SAS Output

```
          2001 Sales for teams under Manager 00121143

                                              Sales for
          Obs    Name                 ID        2001

            3    Elizabeth Spofford   00121060   $1,509
            6    John-Michael Plybon  00121086     $252
            8    Tywanna Mcdade       00121053     $237
           12    Susie Knudson        00121081     $146
           13    Tzue-Ing Cormell     00121100       $0
           14    Daniel Pulliam       00121054     $155
           16    Richard Debank       00121082     $631
           17    Larry Tate           00121094     $657
           18    Glorina Myers        00121051   $1,061
           19    Lionel Wende         00121078      $86
           20    Tingmei Sutton       00121083     $229
```

 **Exercises**

1. **Using Macro Variables to Generate a List Report**

Use macro variables to generate a list report that displays the sales activity of specific groups in a specific month.

a. Examine the descriptor portion of **univ.groupsales2001**.

Partial SAS Output

```
                Alphabetic List of Variables and Attributes

    #    Variable         Type    Len    Format      Informat    Label

    3    EmployeeGroup     Char    40    $10.                     Employee Group
    4    EmployeeHireDate   Num     4    DATE9.      DATE9.       Employee Hire Date
    1    EmployeeID         Char    8                             Employee ID
    2    EmployeeName       Char   40                             Employee Name
    5    OrderDate          Char    9
    6    SaleAmount         Num     8    DOLLAR8.2
```

b. Examine the data portion of **univ.groupsales2001**.

Partial SAS Output

```
                  2001 Sales for teams under Manager 00121143

        Employee                        Employee   Employee                    Sale
 Obs       ID      EmployeeName          Group     HireDate    OrderDate      Amount

   1    00121042   Joseph Robbin-Coker   Clothes   01NOV1995   01-APR-01      $54.70
   2    00121075   Kasha Sugg            Outdoors  01JAN1970   01-JUL-01    $1133.20
   3    00121060   Elizabeth Spofford    Shoes     01JAN1970   01-MAR-01     $227.20
   4    00121056   Stacey Lyszyk         Shoes     01MAY1999   01-MAR-01     $479.70
   5    00121039   Donald Washington     Clothes   01MAY1976   01-SEP-01     $104.60
   6    00121042   Joseph Robbin-Coker   Clothes   01NOV1995   02-APR-01      $65.80
   7    00121074   Eric Michonski        Outdoors  01OCT1984   02-JUL-01      $26.20
   8    00121064   Asishana Polky        Outdoors  01SEP1987   02-JUL-01      $86.80
   9    00121074   Eric Michonski        Outdoors  01OCT1984   02-JUN-01     $519.20
  10    00121043   Sigrid Kagarise       Clothes   01MAR1988   02-MAR-01     $312.10
  11    00121057   Tachaun Voron         Shoes     01DEC1976   02-MAY-01     $115.80
  12    00121064   Asishana Polky        Outdoors  01SEP1987   02-NOV-01      $78.20
```

c. Open the **ch6ex.sas** program into your editor. Then submit the program and view the results.

```
title "Employee Group Clothes' Sales in August 2001";
footnote 'Generated Using SAS for Windows';
proc print data=univ.groupsales2001;
   where EmployeeGroup = 'Clothes' and
         substr(OrderDate,4,6) = 'AUG-01';
run;
```

SAS Output

```
                        Employee Group Clothes' Sales in August 2001

          Employee                          Employee    Employee                      Sale
  Obs       ID        EmployeeName          Group       HireDate    OrderDate        Amount

   46     00121039    Donald Washington     Clothes     01MAY1976   07-AUG-01        $29.20
   52     00121043    Sigrid Kagarise       Clothes     01MAR1988   08-AUG-01       $103.60
   64     00121039    Donald Washington     Clothes     01MAY1976   10-AUG-01       $329.70
   90     00121043    Sigrid Kagarise       Clothes     01MAR1988   14-AUG-01        $37.00
   98     00121042    Joseph Robbin-Coker   Clothes     01NOV1995   16-AUG-01        $54.40
   99     00121042    Joseph Robbin-Coker   Clothes     01NOV1995   16-AUG-01       $132.40
  126     00121041    Jaime Wetherington    Clothes     01JAN1970   22-AUG-01       $189.70
  160     00121043    Sigrid Kagarise       Clothes     01MAR1988   27-AUG-01        $82.40












                                   Generated Using SAS for Windows
```

   d. Create a similar report displaying September 2001 sales for the group named Outdoors. Generalize the program by removing hard-coded values and replacing them with macro variable references.

     1) Add %LET statements and assign the appropriate values to the macro variables **Group** and **Month**.

     2) Add an OPTIONS statement to activate the SYMBOLGEN option.

     3) Modify the TITLE and WHERE statements by replacing hard-coded values with the appropriate macro references.

     4) Modify the FOOTNOTE statement to automatically display the version of SAS and the operating system that are used to generate the report.

SAS Output

```
                          Employee Group Outdoors' Sales in SEP-01

               Employee                          Employee      Employee                       Sale
      Obs        ID       EmployeeName           Group         HireDate    OrderDate        Amount

       70     00121074    Eric Michonski         Outdoors      01OCT1984   10-SEP-01       $177.00
       97     00121075    Kasha Sugg             Outdoors      01JAN1970   15-SEP-01        $19.80
      131     00121064    Asishana Polky         Outdoors      01SEP1987   22-SEP-01        $39.10
      137     00121074    Eric Michonski         Outdoors      01OCT1984   23-SEP-01       $159.10
      168     00121068    Salaheloin Osuba       Outdoors      01SEP1988   28-SEP-01       $200.70




















                             Generated Using SAS 9.1 for WIN
```

✎   Your version and system may differ from the footnote in this output.

The date value in the title is now being displayed differently. The value of **&month** is being used to supply the date value to the title. If you want the date in the title to display as September in the example above, you would either create another macro variable to hold that value, or you can hard-code the value into the title as in the previous program.

6.4 Solutions to Exercises

1. Using Macro Variables to Generate a List Report

```
title;
footnote;

*Exercise 1a;

proc contents data=univ.groupsales2001;
run;

*Exercise 1b;

proc print data=univ.groupsales2001;
run;

*Exercise 1c;

title "Employee Group Clothes' Sales in August 2001";
footnote 'Generated Using SAS for Windows';
proc print data=univ.groupsales2001;
    where EmployeeGroup='Clothes' and
          substr(OrderDate,4,6)='AUG-01';
run;

*Exercise 1d;

%let group=Outdoors;
%let month=SEP-01;

options symbolgen;
title "Employee Group &group' Sales in &month";
footnote "Generated Using SAS &sysver for &sysscp";
proc print data=univ.groupsales2001;
    where EmployeeGroup="&group" and
          substr(OrderDate,4,6)="&month";
run;
```

Chapter 7 Creating and Viewing SAS Data Sets with the SQL Procedure (Self-Study)

7.1   Creating a Report 7-3

7.2   Joining SAS Data Sets 7-7

7.3   Additional SQL Features...7-14

7.4   Solutions to Exercises 7-24

7.1 Creating a Report

Objectives

- Describe how SQL is used in SAS.
- Select columns to be displayed.
- Specify the table to be queried.

3

What Is SQL?

The SQL procedure uses Structured Query Language to perform the following tasks:

- retrieve and manipulate SAS data sets
- create and delete SAS data sets
- generate reports
- add or modify values in a SAS data set
- add, modify, or drop columns in a SAS data set

4

Structured Query Language, or SQL, is a standardized language widely used to retrieve and update data in tables.

Creating a Basic Report

General form of an SQL procedure query to generate output:

```
PROC SQL;
    SELECT variables
        FROM  SAS-data-set;
```

5

The SELECT statement

- retrieves the data by evaluating the query
- formats the selected data into a query result, or report
- displays the report in the OUTPUT destination.

Creating a Basic Report

Create a listing report of product activity.

- Step 1: Invoke the SQL procedure.

```
proc sql;
```

- Step 2: Identify the variables to display on the report.
    Separate the variables with commas.

```
proc sql;
    select CustomerID, CustomerFirstName,
            CustomerLastName
```

6

Creating a Basic Report

■ Step 3: Identify the input data set.

```
proc sql;
   select CustomerID, CustomerFirstName,
          CustomerLastName
      from univ.mastercustomers;
```

■ Step 4: End the procedure with a QUIT statement.

```
proc sql;
   select CustomerID, CustomerFirstName,
          CustomerLastName
      from univ.mastercustomers;
quit;
```

c07s1d1.sas

7

Creating a Basic Report

Partial SAS Output

Customer ID	Customer First Name	Customer Last Name
063432	Wallace	Taiwo
063683	Rick	Ferguson
063848	Marnique	Sanseverino
063897	John	Kibler
064194	Shumaine	Trollo
064756	Jonathon	Restrepo
064810	Randall	Goodman
064940	Glenwood	Hawn
065607	Shihling	Fauver
067000	Dori	Mann
070052	Tonya	Parker
085020	Erik	Rakes
087986	Paul	Causewell
088790	Larry	Mock

8

Creating a Basic Report

c07s1d1.sas

This demonstration illustrates how to create a basic report using the SQL procedure.

```
proc sql;
   select CustomerID, CustomerFirstName,
        CustomerLastName
     from univ.mastercustomers;
quit;
```

Output

```
                         The SAS System
     Customer
     ID            Customer First Name    Customer Last Name

     000492        David                  Dulin
     000551        Blu                    Peachey
     000738        Jerry                  Krejci
     000777        Franklyn               Deverger
     000816        Kerr                   Moorer
     001177        Fay                    Upchurch
     001379        Antwoine               Exelbierd
     002354        Myran                  Husinko
     002734        Dera                   Scarzfava
     002931        Daisy                  Sarsony
     003163        Xuefeng                Leuenberger
     003194        Minette                Godard
     003288        Florentino             Charney
     003370        Jayson                 Gainous
     003386        Nathan                 Watkins
     003837        Joyce                  Hodges
```

7.2 Joining SAS Data Sets

Objectives

- Join two SAS data sets.
- Create a new variable.
- Create a new SAS data set.

11

Join Features

SQL joins have the following characteristics:

- They do not require sorted data.
- They can be performed on up to 32 data sets at one time.
- They allow complex matching criteria using the WHERE clause.

12

Joining Data Sets

General form of an SQL procedure join to generate output:

```
PROC SQL;
    SELECT variables
        FROM SAS-data-set1 AS alias1,
             SAS-data-set2 AS alias2
        WHERE alias1.variable=alias2.variable;
```

13

Joining Data Sets

Create a listing report by joining data sets
univ.mastercustomers and
univ.customerorders by **CustomerID**.

- Step 1: Invoke the SQL procedure and list the variables
  to display.

```
proc sql;
   select CustomerID, CustomerFirstName,
          CustomerLastName, OrderID,
          UnitPrice, Quantity
```

14

Joining Data Sets

■ Step 2: Identify the data sets to join and provide
a table alias for each.

Because **CustomerID** exists in both data sets, identify
which **CustomerID** to use.

```
proc sql;
   select m.CustomerID, CustomerFirstName,
          CustomerLastName, OrderID,
          UnitPrice, Quantity
      from univ.mastercustomers as m,
           univ.customerorders as c
```

15

If you do not identify which **CustomerID** variable you want, an error message occurs.

```
ERROR: Ambiguous reference, column CustomerID is in more than one table.
```

Joining Data Sets

■ Step 3: State the condition on which observations are
matched and terminate the query.

```
proc sql;
   select m.CustomerID, CustomerFirstName,
          CustomerLastName, OrderID,
          UnitPrice, Quantity
      from univ.mastercustomers as m,
           univ.customerorders as c
      where m.CustomerID=c.CustomerID;
quit;
```

c07s2d1.sas

16

The WHERE clause can also be used to subset data.

Joining Data Sets

Partial SAS Output

Customer ID	Customer First Name	Customer Last Name	OrderID	UnitPrice	Quantity
029858	Alice	Maxam	1239347234	130	4
029858	Alice	Maxam	1239686972	122	1
029858	Alice	Maxam	1239686972	468	1
029858	Alice	Maxam	1239686972	87	1
029858	Alice	Maxam	1240124979	181	1
029858	Alice	Maxam	1240437628	135	1
029858	Alice	Maxam	1240541766	23	1
030643	Janet	Domer	1239353107	19	2
030643	Janet	Domer	1239353107	25	2
031116	Lawanna	Massenburg	1240981842	132	2
031116	Lawanna	Massenburg	1240981842	84	2
032096	Tori	Sies	1238338588	63	1
032096	Tori	Sies	1238815024	54	1

17

In this example, the PROC SQL join produces the same result as the DATA step merge. Because the internal process for an SQL join is different from that of a merge, you see different results when

- each key value does not have a match in both data sets
- a many-to-many match occurs.

Creating a New Variable

Create a new variable named **TotSale** by multiplying **Quantity** by **UnitPrice**. Name the new variable **TotSale**.

```
proc sql;
    select m.CustomerID, CustomerFirstName,
           CustomerLastName, OrderID,
           UnitPrice, Quantity,
           Quantity * UnitPrice as TotSale
       from univ.mastercustomers as m,
           univ.customerorders as c
       where m.CustomerID=c.CustomerID;
quit;
```

18   c07s2d2.sas

✎ The new variable is called an *alias*. The AS keyword is required. Omission of the alias causes the column heading to be blank.

Creating a New Variable

Partial SAS Output

Customer ID	Customer First Name	Customer Last Name	Order ID	Unit Price	Quantity	TotSale
064810	Randall	Goodman	1238248877	283	1	283
064810	Randall	Goodman	1238273875	220	1	220
064810	Randall	Goodman	1238768955	52	1	52
064810	Randall	Goodman	1238842450	24	1	24
064810	Randall	Goodman	1239353817	59	2	118
064810	Randall	Goodman	1239489696	11	2	22
064810	Randall	Goodman	1239608721	22	3	66
064810	Randall	Goodman	1239608721	46	3	138
064810	Randall	Goodman	1240590287	21	2	42
065607	Shihling	Fauver	1238209005	267	2	534
065607	Shihling	Fauver	1238590995	158	1	158
065607	Shihling	Fauver	1238590995	19	1	19
065607	Shihling	Fauver	1238730278	106	1	106
065607	Shihling	Fauver	1238898880	140	2	280
065607	Shihling	Fauver	1240454797	12	1	12
065607	Shihling	Fauver	1240703482	171	1	171

19

Creating a SAS Data Set

General form of a PROC SQL query to create
a SAS data set:

```
PROC SQL;
    CREATE TABLE SAS-data-set AS
        SELECT ...
        other SQL clauses;
```

20

The CREATE TABLE statement enables you to store the results of any query in a SAS data set instead of
displaying the query results in the OUTPUT window. In order to see the resulting data set, you must
query it.

Creating a SAS Data Set

Join the tables `univ.mastercustomers` and
`univ.customerorders` to create a new data set.

```
proc sql;
    create table work.ordertotals as
        select m.CustomerID,
                CustomerFirstName,
                CustomerLastName, OrderID,
                UnitPrice, Quantity,
                Quantity*UnitPrice as TotSale
            from univ.mastercustomers as m,
                 univ.customerorders as c
            where m.CustomerID=c.CustomerID;
quit;
```

c07s2d3.sas

21

Creating a New Data Set

c07s2d3.sas

This demonstration illustrates how to create a new data set from a join query.

```
proc sql;
   create table work.ordertotals as
      select m.CustomerID, CustomerFirstName,
         CustomerLastName, OrderID,
         UnitPrice, Quantity,
         Quantity*UnitPrice as TotSale
      from univ.mastercustomers as m,
         univ.customerorders as c
      where m.CustomerID=c.CustomerID;
quit;
```

Partial SAS Log

```
NOTE: Table WORK.ORDERTOTALS created, with 201 rows and 7 columns.
```

7.3 Additional SQL Features

Objectives

- Label column headings.
- Format data values.
- Create a summary report.
- Display the results in sorted order.

24

Enhancing SQL Procedure Reports

General form of an SQL procedure query using labels and formats:

```
PROC SQL;
    SELECT variable LABEL='column-header'
                    FORMAT=format.
        FROM SAS-data-set ;
```

25

Enhancing SQL Procedure Reports

Enhance the previous report.

```
proc sql;
   select m.CustomerID,
          CustomerFirstName format=$10.,
          CustomerLastName format=$15.,
          OrderID,
          UnitPrice format=dollar7.2,
          Quantity,
          Quantity * UnitPrice as TotSale
                format=dollar8.2
                label='Total Sale Amount'
       from univ.mastercustomers as m,
            univ.customerorders as c
       where m.CustomerID=c.CustomerID;
quit;
```

c07s3d1.sas

26

Enhancing SQL Procedure Reports

Partial Output

Customer ID	Customer First Name	Customer Last Name	OrderID	Unit Price	Quantity	Sale Amount
062096	Craig	Knapmeyer	1240062267	$36.00	3	$108.00
062096	Craig	Knapmeyer	1240832690	$27.00	4	$108.00
062284	Robert	Britt	1238409388	$15.00	1	$15.00
062284	Robert	Britt	1238409388	$33.00	1	$33.00
064810	Randall	Goodman	1238248877	$175.00	4	$700.00
064810	Randall	Goodman	1238248877	$283.00	1	$283.00
064810	Randall	Goodman	1238273875	$220.00	1	$220.00
064810	Randall	Goodman	1238768955	$52.00	1	$52.00
064810	Randall	Goodman	1238842450	$24.00	1	$24.00
064810	Randall	Goodman	1239353817	$59.00	2	$118.00
064810	Randall	Goodman	1239489696	$11.00	2	$22.00
064810	Randall	Goodman	1239608721	$22.00	3	$66.00
064810	Randall	Goodman	1239608721	$46.00	3	$138.00
064810	Randall	Goodman	1240590287	$21.00	2	$42.00

27

Customizing a Report

c07s3d1.sas

This demonstration illustrates how to customize a report with labels and formats.

```
proc sql;
   select m.CustomerID,
          CustomerFirstName format=$10.,
          CustomerLastName format=$15.,
          OrderID,
          UnitPrice format=dollar7.2,
          Quantity,
          Quantity*UnitPrice as TotSale
                     format=dollar8.2
                     label='Total Sale Amount'
      from univ.mastercustomers as m,
           univ.customerorders as c
      where m.CustomerID=c.CustomerID;
quit;
```

Partial Output

```
                                     The SAS System


                                                                   Total
                                                                    Sale
 Customer  Customer  Customer
 ID        First Name Last Name    OrderID     UnitPrice  Quantity  Amount

 060308    Boyden    Barrosa      1238954477    $35.00       1      $35.00
 060577    Gemina    Ross         1239481532    $24.00       3      $72.00
 060577    Gemina    Ross         1239481532    $39.00       3     $117.00
 060577    Gemina    Ross         1239481532   $105.00       2     $210.00
 060577    Gemina    Ross         1240243513    $39.00       1      $39.00
 060577    Gemina    Ross         1240268147    $63.00       1      $63.00
 060994    Vipul     Furches      1239940635    $85.00       1      $85.00
 060994    Vipul     Furches      1239940635    $24.00       2      $48.00
 060994    Vipul     Furches      1240606925    $19.00       1      $19.00
 061243    Marvin    Staton       1238720735   $107.00       1     $107.00
 061243    Marvin    Staton       1239923717    $28.00       2      $56.00
 061243    Marvin    Staton       1240792996   $106.00       1     $106.00
 061243    Marvin    Staton       1240998390    $40.00       1      $40.00
 061347    Stacey    Wishum       1240139411    $39.00       1      $39.00
```

Creating Summary Reports

General form of an SQL procedure query to generate summary output:

```
PROC SQL;
    SELECT group-variable,
            SUM(analysis-variable)
    FROM SAS-data-set
    GROUP BY group-variable;
```

If a summary function is used in the SELECT clause with only one argument, then an overall statistic is calculated down the column.

29

If more than one argument is specified in the summary function, the calculation is performed for each row, as in the DATA step.

If a GROUP BY clause appears in the statement and a summary function is used in the SELECT clause, the statistic is calculated down the column for each unique value of the grouping variable(s).

Creating Summary Reports

- Step 1: Identify the variables to display, the input data sets, and the matching criteria.

```
proc sql;
   select m.CustomerID,
          CustomerFirstName format=$10.,
          CustomerLastName format=$15.,
          sum(Quantity) label= 'Total Quantity',
          sum(Quantity*UnitPrice) as TotSale
                  format=dollar12.2
                  label='Total Sale Amount'
      from univ.mastercustomers as m,
           univ.customerorders as c
      where m.CustomerID=c.CustomerID;
```

30

Creating Summary Reports

- Step 2: Identify the grouping variable(s).

```
proc sql;
   select m.CustomerID,
          CustomerFirstName format=$10.,
          CustomerLastName format=$15.,
          sum(Quantity) label='Total Quantity',
          sum(Quantity*UnitPrice) as TotSale
             format=dollar12.2
             label='Total Amount Purchased'
      from univ.mastercustomers as m,
           univ.customerorders as c
      where m.CustomerID=c.CustomerID
      group by m.CustomerID, CustomerFirstName,
             CustomerLastName;
quit;
```

31   c07s3d2.sas

Creating Summary Reports

Partial Output

```
                         The SAS System

   Customer  Customer     Customer          Total  Total Amount
   ID        First Name   Last Name      Quantity     Purchased

   029858    Alice        Maxam                10     $1,536.00
   030643    Janet        Domer                 4        $88.00
   031116    Lawanna      Massenburg            4       $432.00
   032096    Tori         Sies                 26     $3,531.00
   033113    Richard      Mcgee                 2       $252.00
   033312    Brent        Zei                   6       $752.00
   033369    Li           Trone                 4       $104.00
   035668    Denise       Dion                  5       $373.00
   035901    James        Chmelar              13     $1,225.00
   036324    Tinker       Hitesman             14     $1,057.00
   036355    Nobuhiko     Mcmillian             2       $196.00
   036732    Cindi        Mcquay-Smith          7       $704.00
   037971    Anthony      Russell               5       $276.00
```

32

Ordering the Report

General form of an SQL procedure query to generate ordered output:

PROC SQL;
    SELECT *group-variable*,
           SUM(*analysis-variable*)
    FROM *SAS-data-set*
    GROUP BY *group-variable*
    ORDER BY *variable1 <, variable2>* ;

The default is ascending order.

33

Ordering the Report

Order the report by total sale.

```
proc sql;
   select m.CustomerID,
          CustomerFirstName format=$10.,
          CustomerLastName format=$15.,
          sum(Quantity) label='Total Quantity',
          sum(Quantity*UnitPrice) as TotSale
               format=dollar12.2
               label='Total Amount Purchased'
      from univ.mastercustomers as m,
           univ.customerorders as c
      where m.CustomerID=c.CustomerID
      group by m.CustomerID, CustomerFirstName,
               CustomerLastName
      order by TotSale;
quit;
```

c07s3d3.sas

34

Ordering the Report

Partial output

```
                        The SAS System

Customer   Customer    Customer            Total   Total Amount
ID         First Name  Last Name        Quantity      Purchased

060308     Boyden      Barrosa                 1         $35.00
049048     Ryan        Mckinney                2         $38.00
061347     Stacey      Wishum                  1         $39.00
044817     Devinder    Zezefellis              1         $43.00
055039     Wiegand     Elliott-Smith           1         $48.00
062284     Robert      Britt                   2         $48.00
048443     Stanton     Fedynskyj-Slysh         2         $50.00
047629     Eugene      Hart                    2         $70.00
043358     Carl        White                   2         $80.00
030643     Janet       Domer                   4         $88.00
033369     Li          Trone                   4        $104.00
```

35

Creating a Summary Report

c07s3d3.sas

This demonstration illustrates how to create a summary report in order by total sale.

```
proc sql;
   select   m.CustomerID,
            CustomerFirstName format=$10.,
            CustomerLastName format=$15.,
            sum(Quantity) label='Total Quantity',
            sum(Quantity*UnitPrice) as TotSale
                    format=dollar12.2
                    label='Total Amount Purchased'
       from univ.mastercustomers as m,
            univ.customerorders as c
       where a.CustomerID=c.CustomerID
       group by m.CustomerID, CustomerFirstName,
            CustomerLastName
       order by TotSale;
quit;
```

Partial SAS Output

The SAS System

Customer ID	Customer First Name	Customer Last Name	Total Quantity	Total Amount Purchased
060308	Boyden	Barrosa	1	$35.00
049048	Ryan	Mckinney	2	$38.00
061347	Stacey	Wishum	1	$39.00
044817	Devinder	Zezefellis	1	$43.00
055039	Wiegand	Elliott-Smith	1	$48.00
062284	Robert	Britt	2	$48.00
048443	Stanton	Fedynskyj-Slysh	2	$50.00
047629	Eugene	Hart	2	$70.00
043358	Carl	White	2	$80.00
030643	Janet	Domer	4	$88.00
033369	Li	Trone	4	$104.00
060994	Vipul	Furches	4	$152.00
038812	Obie	Flook	2	$154.00
036355	Nobuhiko	Mcmillian	2	$196.00
044108	Howard	Derbyshire	1	$240.00
051347	Madhu	Schacher	5	$242.00
033113	Richard	Mcgee	2	$252.00
058892	William	Alford	8	$264.00
037971	Anthony	Russell	5	$276.00
061243	Marvin	Staton	5	$309.00
048540	Maristene	Scarfone	7	$323.00
035668	Denise	Dion	5	$373.00

 **Exercises**

1. Creating a List Report

Create a list report of the sales by employees from 1999 through 2002. Display the employee ID, employee group, total amount sold, the difference in sales between 2001 and 2002, and the average sales for 1999 through 2002.

- Join **univ.totsales** and **univ.totsales2002** by the employee ID, which has a different name in each data set.

- Create a new variable **SalesTotals** by adding the variables **TotSales1999**, **TotSales2000**, **TotSales2001**, and **TotSales2002**.

- Create the new variable **SalesDifference** by taking the difference between **TotSales2001** and **TotSales2002**.

- Create the new variable **AvgSales** by taking the average of **TotSales1999**, **TotSales2000**, **TotSales2001**, and **TotSales2002**.

- Use labels and formats to enhance the report.

- Include the ORDER BY clause to display the sales by **EmployeeGroup** and **EmployeeID**.

Partial Output

```
                               The SAS System

                                                Difference in      Average
   Employee                      Total Sales for  Sales between   Sales from
   ID       Employee Group        1999 - 2002    2001 and 2002   1999 - 2002
   ─────────────────────────────────────────────────────────────────────────
   00121020  Assorted Sports Articles   $6,844.60      $3,259.00    $1,711.15
   00121021  Assorted Sports Articles   $4,991.00      $2,446.70    $1,247.75
   00121024  Assorted Sports Articles   $1,523.80        $227.20      $380.95
   00121025  Assorted Sports Articles   $8,288.80      $1,628.10    $2,072.20
   00121027  Children Sports            $1,161.40        $374.30      $290.35
   00121029  Children Sports            $1,998.80        $659.00      $499.70
   00121030  Children Sports            $2,042.60        $478.00      $510.65
   00121031  Children Sports            $1,422.80        $436.60      $355.70
   00121033  Children Sports              $920.40        $350.30      $230.10
   00121035  Children Sports            $2,830.76        $738.78      $707.69
   00121037  Clothes                    $8,446.76      $2,028.38    $2,111.69
   00121039  Clothes                    $9,109.80      $1,832.40    $2,277.45
   00121040  Clothes                    $8,790.60      $2,389.30    $2,197.65
   00121041  Clothes                    $7,724.40      $3,436.30    $1,931.10
   00121042  Clothes                    $9,001.40      $2,053.20    $2,250.35
   00121043  Clothes                   $11,035.60      $2,653.20    $2,758.90
   00121044  Clothes                    $9,286.50      $2,776.25    $2,321.63
   00121051  Golf                       $2,988.00        $433.00      $747.00
```

2. Creating a Summary Report

Modify the previous program to create a summary report that displays the total sales for each employee group.

- Include only the existing column named **EmployeeGroup** in the SELECT clause.

- Create the new variable **SalesDifference** by taking the difference between **TotSales2001** and **TotSales2002**. Hint: You can use **sum(TotSales2002 - TotSales2001)**.

- Specify **EmployeeGroup** as the group variable.

Output

```
                        The SAS System
                                          Difference in
                                          Sales between
                 Employee Group           2001 and 2002

                 Assorted Sports Articles      $7,561.00
                 Children Sports               $3,036.98
                 Clothes                      $17,169.03
                 Golf                            $433.00
                 Indoor Sports                 $2,356.30
                 Outdoors                     $15,404.88
                 Racket Sports                   $800.60
                 Running - Jogging             $2,893.20
                 Shoes                        $11,154.40
                 Swim Sports                     $218.90
                 Team Sports                   $1,421.75
                 Winter Sports                 $5,265.53
```

7.4 Solutions to Exercises

1. Creating a List Report

```
proc sql;
   select EmployeeId,
          a.EmployeeGroup format=$25.,
          sum(TotSales1999,TotSales2000,TotSales2001,TotSales2002)
                  as SalesTotals format=dollar16.2
                                 label='Total Sales for 1999 - 2002',
          (TotSales2002 - TotSales2001)
                  as SalesDifference format=dollar15.2
                      label='Difference in Sales between 2001 and 2002',
          mean(TotSales1999, TotSales2000, TotSales2001,TotSales2002)
                  as AvgSales format=dollar12.2
                                 label='Average Sales from 1999 - 2002'
      from univ.totsales as a,
           univ.totsales2002 as b
      where a.EmployeeId=b.EmpId
      order by a.EmployeeGroup, EmployeeID;
quit;
```

You can also calculate the total sales by typing the code below. However, the SUM function ignores missing values; the + does not. Your results could vary between the two methods.

```
(TotSales1999+TotSales2000+TotSales2001+TotSales2002) as SalesTotals
```

2. Creating a Summary Report

```
proc sql;
   select a.EmployeeGroup format=$25.,
          sum(TotSales2002 - TotSales2001) as SalesDifference
                    format=dollar15.2
                    label='Difference in Sales between 2001 and 2002'

      from univ.totsales as a,
           univ.totsales2002 as b
      where a.EmployeeId=b.EmpId
      group by a.EmployeeGroup;
quit;
```

Appendix A Index

%

%LET statement, 6-22–6-28
  syntax, 6-22
%PUT statement, 6-12
  syntax, 6-12

A

analysis variable, 2-13
array processing, 3-59–3-66
ARRAY statement
  syntax, 3-61
assignment statement
  syntax, 3-16
automatic macro variables, 6-14–6-21
  displaying, 6-17

B

bar chart
  creating, 2-7–2-9
  horizontal, 2-6
  using formats, 2-14
  vertical, 2-5
browsing the data portion, 1-39
browsing the descriptor portion, 1-38

C

CAXIS= option
  PLOT statement, 2-27
character constant, 3-17
character functions, 3-23
character values, 3-51–3-52
chart variable, 2-5
COLOR= option
  FOOTNOTE statement, 2-15
  TITLE statement, 2-15
combining data sets, 4-3–4-5
comparison operators, 3-33–3-34
compilation phase, 1-34
COMPRESS function, 3-24
concatenating data sets, 4-3–4-6
conditional processing, 6-6
conditional statements, 3-32
constants

character, 3-17
  numeric, 3-17
CONTENTS procedure
  syntax, 1-38
CREATE TABLE statement, 7-12
creating summary SQL reports, 7-17–7-20
CTEXT= option
  PLOT statement, 2-27

D

data
  processing, 3-47–3-52
data portion
  browsing, 1-39
  SAS data set, 1-15
data relationships, 4-16
data sets
  combining, 4-3–4-5
  concatenating, 4-3–4-6
  interleaving, 4-7–4-13
  joining, 7-7–7-9
  sorting, 4-8–4-9
DATA statement, 1-4–1-5, 1-26–1-27
  syntax, 1-27
  VIEW= option syntax, 1-63
DATA step, 1-4–1-5, 1-24
  compiling, 1-34
  components of, 1-8
  DATA statement, 1-26
  executing, 1-36–1-38
  INFILE statement, 1-26
  INPUT statement, 1-26
  RUN statement, 1-26
  syntax, 1-33, 3-5
DATA step concatenation
  syntax, 4-5
DATA step file, 1-61
DATA step view, 1-62
  advantages, 1-66
data-driven applications, 6-7
date functions, 3-22
DBMS table
  reading, 5-3–5-15
DESCRIBE statement
  syntax, 1-63

descriptor portion
  browsing, 1-38
  SAS data set, 1-14
DISCRETE option, 2-11
displaying automatic macro variables, 6-17
displaying macro variable values, 6-10–6-13
displaying system information, 6-5
DO loop
  incrementing, 3-47–3-48
  syntax, 3-49
DO loops, 3-47–3-52
DO statement
  syntax, 3-39
DROP= data set option
  syntax, 3-6

E

END statement
  syntax, 3-39
execution phase, 1-36–1-38
expressions, 3-17

F

FIND function, 3-23
FONT= option
  FOOTNOTE statement, 2-15
  TITLE statement, 2-15
FOOTNOTE statement
  COLOR= option, 2-15
  FONT= option, 2-15
  HEIGHT= option, 2-15
FORMAT statement, 1-41
formatted input, 1-28
functions
  COMPRESS, 3-24
  INTNX, 3-21
  MDY, 3-22
  MEAN, 3-25
  MONTH, 3-21
  QTR, 3-21
  SUBSTR, 3-24
  SUM, 3-25
  TODAY, 3-22
  WEEKDAY, 3-22
  YEAR, 3-21

G

GCHART procedure
  syntax, 2-4
global macro variables, 6-8

GPLOT procedure
  syntax, 2-20

H

HAXIS= option
  PLOT statement, 2-27
HBAR statement, 2-4
HEIGHT= option
  FOOTNOTE statement, 2-15
horizontal bar chart, 2-6

I

IF-THEN ELSE statement
  syntax, 3-32
IN= data set option
  syntax, 4-19
INFILE statement, 1-26–1-27
  syntax, 1-27
informats, 1-29–1-31
INPUT statement, 1-26–1-27
  syntax, 1-28
interleaving, 4-7
interleaving data sets, 4-7–4-13
INTNX function, 3-21

J

join features, 7-7
joining data sets, 7-7–7-9

K

KEEP= data set option
  syntax, 3-6

L

LABEL statement, 2-29
  syntax, 1-45
LENGTH statement
  syntax, 3-37
LIBNAME statement
  syntax, 1-21
libref
  SAS data library, 1-19
logical operators, 3-34–3-35

M

macro facility
  purpose, 6-4
macro variable values

displaying, 6-10–6-13
macro variables
    automatic, 6-14–6-21
    global, 6-8
    referencing, 6-8–6-10
macro-based programs, 6-7
many-to-many relationship, 4-16
match-merging, 4-17–4-24
    syntax, 4-17
MDY function, 3-22
MEAN function, 3-25
missing data values, 1-16
MONTH function, 3-21

N

numeric constant, 3-17
numeric values, 3-51–3-52

O

one-to-many relationship, 4-16
one-to-one relationship, 4-16
operators, 3-18
    comparison, 3-33–3-34
    logical, 3-34–3-35

P

parenthesis, 3-18
pie chart, 2-6
    creating, 2-7–2-9
PIE statement, 2-4
PLOT statement
    CAXIS= option, 2-27
    CTEXT= option, 2-27
    HAXIS= option, 2-27
    VAXIS= option, 2-27
PRINT procedure
    syntax, 1-39
PROC statement, 1-6–1-7
PROC step, 1-6–1-7
    components of, 1-9
procedures
    CONTENTS, 1-38
    PRINT, 1-39
    SORT, 4-8
processing data, 3-47–3-52

Q

QTR function, 3-21

R

RENAME= data set option
    syntax, 4-21
repetitive processing, 6-6
RUN statement, 1-33
RUN statement, 1-8–1-11, 1-26
    syntax, 1-33
RUN-group processing, 2-14

S

SAS data file, 1-60
SAS data library, 1-18–1-20
    libref, 1-19
    permanent, 1-20
    temporary, 1-19
SAS data set, 1-60
    creating, 3-3–3-13, 7-12–7-13
    data portion, 1-15
    descriptor portion, 1-14
    naming, 1-17
    reading, 3-3–3-5
    SAS file, 1-13
SAS data set, temporary
    creating, 1-18
SAS date values, 1-16, 1-31
SAS file
    SAS data set, 1-13
SAS filename
    syntax, 1-22
SAS formats, 1-41–1-46
SAS function
    syntax, 3-19
    using, 3-20
SAS informats, 1-29–1-31
SAS program
    components, 1-4
SCAN function, 3-23
scatter plots
    producing, 2-24–2-25
SELECT statement, 7-4
selecting variables, 3-6–3-8
SET statement, 3-4
SORT procedure
    syntax, 4-8
sorting a data set, 4-8–4-9
special operators, 3-78–3-79
SQL (Structured Query Language), 7-3
SQL joins
    features, 7-7
SQL procedure

SELECT statement, 7-4
summary reports, 7-17–7-20
syntax, 7-4
syntax to create a SAS data set, 7-12
syntax to generate ordered output, 7-19
syntax to generate output, 7-4, 7-8
syntax to generate summary output, 7-17
syntax using labels and formats, 7-14
SQL reports
   enhancing, 7-14–7-17
statement, 1-8
statements
   %LET, 6-22–6-28
   %PUT, 6-12
   ARRAY, 3-61
   assignment, 3-17
   conditional, 3-32
   DATA, 1-8–1-10, 1-26–1-27, 1-63
   DESCRIBE, 1-63
   IF-THEN ELSE, 3-32
   INFILE, 1-26–1-27
   INPUT, 1-26–1-27, 1-28–1-32
   LIBNAME, 1-21
   PROC, 1-6–1-7
   RUN, 1-8–1-11, 1-26
   SELECT, 7-4
   SET, 3-4
   subsetting IF, 3-71
   WHERE, 3-77
steps
   components of, 1-7
Structured Query Language (SQL), 7-3
subsetting IF statement
   syntax, 3-71
SUM function, 3-25
summary SQL reports
   creating, 7-17–7-20
summary statistic, 2-12
SYMBOL statement
   cancelling, 2-27
   syntax, 2-21
SYMBOL statement options, 2-22–2-23, 2-26

SYMBOLGEN system option
   syntax, 6-11
syntax rules, 1-9–1-11
system information
   displaying, 6-5

T

temporary SAS data set
   creating, 1-18
TITLE statement
   COLOR= option, 2-15
   FONT= option, 2-15
   HEIGHT= option, 2-15
TODAY function, 3-22

U

UPCASE function, 3-23

V

values
   character, 3-51–3-52
   numeric, 3-51–3-52
variables
   creating, 7-11
   naming, 1-17
   selecting, 3-6–3-8
VAXIS= option
   PLOT statement, 2-27
VBAR statement, 2-4
vertical bar chart, 2-5
VIEW= option
   syntax in DATA statement, 1-63

W

WEEKDAY function, 3-22
WHERE statement
   syntax, 3-77

Y

YEAR function, 3-21